COOL RESTAURANTS

TOP OF THE WORLD
VOLUME 2

Edited by
Martin Nicholas Kunz
& Raphael Guillou

teNeues

Contents

New York
STK Midtown
abc kitchen
Delicatessen
Ember Room
The Wright
Beauty & Essex

San Francisco
Gitane

Vancouver
Hawksworth Restaurant

Philadelphia
Distrito

Las Vegas
Beijing Noodle No. 9

Los Angeles
Delphine

Mexico City
Tori Tori

São Paulo
Empório Baglioni

Copenhagen
Kødbyens Fiskebar

Berlin
Long March Canteen
Sage Restaurant

Åndalsnes
Troll Wall Restaurant

Vienna
Neni am Naschmarkt
Plachuttas Gasthaus zur Oper

Paris
Mandarin Oriental Paris

London
Barbican Foodhall and Lounge

Stockholm
Griffins' Steakhouse Extraordinaire

Strasbourg
La Corde à Linge

Bucharest
Lacrimi si Sfinti

Mumbai
Tote on the Turf
Blue Frog

Tokyo
Alice of Magic World
+green

Madrid
La Terraza del Casino

Seongnam
Namus Boutique Restaurant

Yamanashi
Hōtō Fudō

Thessaloniki
Chan at The Met Hotel

Herzliya
Zozobra

Beirut
Iris
Momo at the Souks

New Delhi
Smoke House Deli

Mykonos
Alemàgou

Hong Kong
SEVVA
208 Duecento Otto
Ozone
Fairwood Buddies Café

Dubai
At.mosphere

Mahé
Konoba

Singapore
Jing

Stellenbosch
Makaron

Cape Town
Cape to Cuba

Sydney
Concrete Blonde

A matter of taste

Take a vacant space, add a handful of furniture and a capable chef, stir thoroughly and voilà—a new restaurant is born.

Some will always swear by the rustic Italian restaurant on the corner whose aging illuminated sign invites you into a world of white paper tablecloths, potted plants, and deceptively realistic marble busts. Here, the restaurant owner reigns supreme, and when the mood strikes and he has a few glasses of Chianti under his belt, he might treat diners to an almost stage-worthy rendition of "O sole mio." Perfection in terms of furnishings is of secondary importance; what matters are the atmosphere and a plate of your favorite pasta that tastes as if "la mamma" had prepared it herself. Fans of this inimitable blend of nostalgia, down-to-earth ambience, and a dash of wanderlust describe it as authentic. In other words, "You know what you're getting!"

To excite modern-day guests, however, you need far more than authenticity and honest food. Apart from culinary standards, today's clientele is increasingly interested in design and has ever higher expectations when it comes to the overall restaurant concept and interior design. The title "world class" is attainable only if a restaurant makes a lasting impression on its diners' sense of taste while also appealing to their sense of aesthetics and design. As a result, the work of architects and interior, graphic, and lighting designers has taken on new significance, and a consistent corporate identity is just as important as the skills of the chef. Consistency in every detail creates a setting that immerses guests in another world during their visit.

This book features 47 restaurants from around the globe; each, in its own unique way, is one of the coolest restaurants in the world. These multifaceted restaurants stand out from the crowd: In Norway, a simple cafeteria such as the Troll Wall Restaurant becomes an experience thanks to the architecture of its glass façade that opens up onto a breathtaking mountain panorama. At At.mosphere in Dubai, on the other hand, diners can enjoy a steak at an elevation of 1,450 feet: The restaurant is located in Burj Khalifa, the highest building of the world. The chefs at Hawksworth Restaurant and La Terraza del Casino are considered visionaries in their field; their genius is reflected not only in the creations they plate but in the entire interior of their restaurants. At Tori Tori in Mexico City, corporate design was carried to the extreme, resulting in a building and all its interior furnishings being constructed specifically for this Japanese restaurant. Despite a tendency towards futuristic themes, designers and restaurateurs continue to find inspiration in tradition and history. Delicatessen offers a new interpretation of the classic American deli, while Cape to Cuba in South Africa is a lavish homage to Che Guevara and Hemingway.

No recipe in the world can tell you how many ingredients you need for the perfect restaurant and what the proper proportions of design, food, architecture, lighting, sound, and numerous other elements should be. One thing holds true, however: In the end, it is simply a matter of taste—and taste is something that has always provided fodder for animated discussions.

Raphael Guillou

Eine Frage des Geschmacks

Man nehme: ein leerstehendes Lokal, eine Handvoll Mobiliar sowie einen fähigen Küchenchef, rühre einmal kräftig um und voilà – fertig ist das Restaurant.

Sicher, so manch einer schwört noch immer auf den urigen Italiener an der Ecke, dessen etwas betagte Leuchtreklame einlädt in eine Welt aus weißen Papiertischdecken, Topfpflanzen und täuschend echten Marmorbüsten, regiert von einem Restaurantbesitzer, der bei guter Laune und einigen Gläsern Chianti ein beinahe bühnenreifes „O sole mio" zum Besten gibt. Perfektion in puncto Einrichtung ist dabei eher zweitrangig; was zählt, ist die Atmosphäre und ein Teller der Lieblingspasta, die schmeckt als hätte sie „la Mamma" gerade höchstpersönlich zubereitet. Als authentisch bezeichnen Liebhaber diese unnachahmliche Mischung aus Nostalgie, Bodenständigkeit und einer Prise Fernweh. Mit anderen Worten: „Da weiß man, was man hat!"

Um die Gäste von heute zu begeistern, braucht es jedoch weitaus mehr als Authentizität und ehrliches Essen. Eine zunehmend an Design interessierte Klientel stellt immer höhere Ansprüche, die neben dem kulinarischen Niveau vor allem dem Gesamtkonzept und einem passenden Interieur gelten. Das Prädikat „Weltklasse" rückt erst dann in greifbare Nähe, wenn nicht nur der Geschmackssinn, sondern auch die Rezeptoren für Ästhetik und Design nachhaltig beeindruckt sind. Die Arbeit von Architekten, Interior Designern, Grafikern oder Lichtgestaltern erhält dadurch einen neuen Stellenwert, und eine stimmige Corporate Identity ist mindestens so wichtig wie das Können des Küchenchefs. Konsequent bis ins Detail wird so eine Inszenierung geschaffen, die den Gast für die Zeit des Besuchs in eine andere Welt abtauchen lässt.

Dieses Buch zeigt 47 Restaurants rund um den Globus, jedes auf seine ganz individuelle Weise eines der coolsten der Welt. Facettenreich heben sie sich von der Masse ab: In Norwegen wird eine einfache Cafeteria wie das Troll Wall Restaurant durch die gläserne Architektur und ein atemberaubendes Bergpanorama zum Erlebnis. In Dubai dagegen genießt man im At.mosphere sein Steak auf 442 Metern Höhe, und zwar im Burj Khalifa, dem höchsten Gebäude der Welt. Die Küchenchefs des Hawksworth Restaurants oder des La Terraza del Casino gehören zu den Visionären ihres Metiers, was sich nicht nur in den Kreationen auf dem Teller, sondern im gesamten Interieur widerspiegelt. Im Fall des Tori Tori in Mexico City wurde die Idee des Corporate Designs auf die Spitze getrieben und ein Gebäude inklusive allen Mobiliars eigens für das japanische Restaurant erbaut. Trotz einer Tendenz zu futuristischen Themen lassen sich Gestalter und Gastronomen immer wieder von Tradition und Geschichte inspirieren. Eine Neuinterpretation des amerikanischen Delis liefert das Delicatessen, während das südafrikanische Cape to Cuba als eine üppig dekorierte Hommage an Che Guevara und Hemingway erinnert.

Wie viele Zutaten man für das perfekte Restaurant benötigt und in welchem Mengenverhältnis Design, Essen, Architektur, Licht, Sound etc. zueinander stehen müssen, verrät kein Rezept dieser Welt. Eines ist jedoch sicher: Letztlich ist es eine Frage des Geschmacks, und über den lässt sich ja bekanntlich streiten.

Raphael Guillou

Tout est une question de goût !

Prenez un local vide, ajoutez-y une poignée de meubles et un chef talentueux, mélangez le tout avec finesse et voilà ! Votre restaurant est prêt.

Bien sûr, il y aura toujours ceux qui ne jureront que par l'italien du coin, dont la vieille affiche lumineuse invite à venir découvrir un monde rustique fait de nappes en papier blanches, de plantes empotées et de bustes en marbre imité, où le propriétaire vous chantera un « O sole mio » digne d'un « castrato » dans une atmosphère de bonne humeur, après quelques verres de Chianti. La perfection de l'aménagement est ici secondaire ; ce qui compte, c'est l'ambiance et le plat de pâtes tel que « la mamma » le prépare. Les amateurs de ce genre d'endroit qualifient d'authentique ce mélange de nostalgie des contrées lointaines et d'éléments conservateurs, simples et traditionnels. En d'autres mots : « Ici, on sait à quoi s'attendre ! ».

Mais aujourd'hui, la clientèle attend bien plus que de l'authenticité et de la cuisine traditionnelle. Ses attentes en ce qui concerne le design, l'aménagement intérieur et le niveau culinaire sont de plus en plus élevées. On gagne l' « élite mondiale » lorsque l'on propose un concept qui non seulement éveille les papilles, mais séduit également par son esthétisme et son design. Il ne suffit plus de disposer des talents culinaires d'un grand chef. L'identité visuelle, créée par les architectes, designers d'intérieur, graphistes et spécialistes d'aménagement lumineux est aujourd'hui devenue indispensable. Rien ne séduit plus la clientèle que de la transporter dans un autre monde le temps de sa visite.

Cet ouvrage vous fait découvrir 47 restaurants du monde entier qui, chacun à leur manière, présentent un charme très particulier. Leur diversité les rend inoubliables : l'édifice en verre de cette simple cafétéria norvégienne, le Troll Wall Restaurant, vous plonge dans un décor de montagnes à couper le souffle. A Dubaï, vous dégusterez votre steak à 442 mètres de hauteur dans le restaurant At.mosphere, logé dans la tour la plus haute du monde. Les grands chefs du Hawksworth Restaurant ou de La Terraza del Casino comptent parmi les grands visionnaires de leur métier si l'on considère l'innovation des plats et de l'aménagement intérieur. Le Tori Tori de Mexico symbolise le concept du « Corporate Design » par excellence grâce à un édifice et un mobilier spécialement conçus pour ce restaurant japonais. Malgré un goût prononcé pour les concepts futuristes, décorateurs et gastronomes ne renoncent pas à s'inspirer des tendances anciennes et traditionnelles. Le Delicatessen vous fait ainsi redécouvrir les « Delis » américains pendant que le restaurant sud-africain Cape to Cuba rend hommage au Che Guevara et à Hemingway.

Quant à connaître le dosage adéquat de design, d'art culinaire, d'architecture, de lumière ou de quelque autre ingrédient permettant de concocter le restaurant parfait, aucune recette au monde ne vous livrera la clé. Une chose est sûre : tout est une question de goût, et chacun a son mot à dire à ce sujet !

Raphael Guillou

Zozobra

Herzliya, Israel

Arieh Shenkar 7
Herzliya, 46725

Phone: +972 9 957 7077
www.zozobra.co.il

Prices: $$
Cuisine: Asian

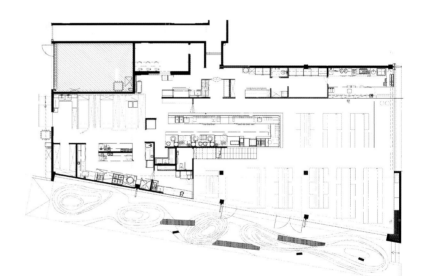

Architecture/Design
Baranowitz Kronenberg Architecture
www.bkarc.com

Photos
Amit Geron

Located in the town of Herzliya in Israel, the video projections on the wall of this Asian noodle bar make it look more like a club than a restaurant. Architects Alon Baranowitz and Irene Kronenberg from Tel Aviv handled the interior design, the centerpiece of which is an impressive ceiling element. Above the bar, it shimmers in different shades of gray like a geometrically shaped crystal. Narrow, cylindrical LED spotlights above the tables form a contrast with the bulky contour of this geometric structure. The furniture has a minimalist design. Dishes prepared in an open stainless steel kitchen are served at sleek tables and benches. There's no privacy to be found here; instead, the architects designed the space to encourage interaction among diners.

Die Videoprojektionen an der Wand lassen die asiatische Nudel-Bar im israelischen Städtchen Herzliya eher wie einen Club als wie ein Restaurant aussehen. Die Architekten Alon Baranowitz und Irene Kronenberg aus Tel Aviv haben die Einrichtung gestaltet, deren Kernstück ein imposantes Deckenelement ist. Es schimmert in verschiedenen Grautönen und thront wie ein geometrisch geformter Kristall über der Bar. Einen Kontrast zu seiner massigen Kontur bilden die schmalen, zylinderförmigen LED-Spots über den Tischen. Die Möbel sind puristisch designt. An schlichten Tischen und Bänken werden Gerichte serviert, die zuvor in der offenen Edelstahl-Küche zubereitet wurden. Privatsphäre? Fehlanzeige. Der Raum soll zum Austausch und zur Interaktion einladen, finden die Architekten.

Les vidéos projetées au mur donnent au bar à nouilles asiatique situé dans la petite ville israélienne de Herzliya des allures de boîte de nuit plutôt que de restaurant. Le plafond est le joyau de la décoration effectuée par les architectes de Tel Aviv Alon Baranowitz et Irene Kronenberg. Une imposante structure géométrique brille en effet de mille lueurs grises au-dessus du bar, tel du cristal. En comparaison de ses contours massifs, les fines lampes LEDs cylindriques qui éclairent les tables paraissent minuscules. Le design du mobilier se veut épuré et les plats préparés dans la cuisine ouverte en acier fin sont servis à des tables et des bancs très simples. Les architectes ont à dessein créé une salle invitant à l'échange et à l'interaction, aussi est-il inutile d'y chercher l'intimité.

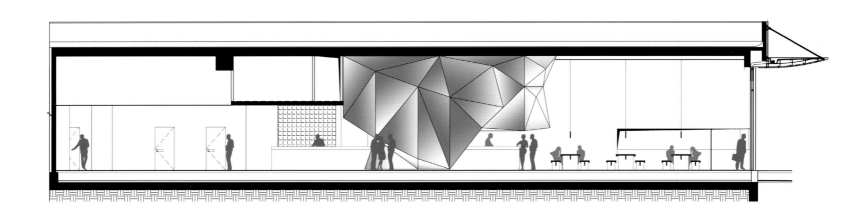

Iris

Beirut, Lebanon

Rooftop of the An-Nahar Building, Martyrs' Square
Beirut, 01-983008

Phone: +961 3 090 936
www.irisbeirut.com

Prices: $$$
Cuisine: Fusion

Architecture/Design
Suzy Nasr & .PSLAB
www.suzynasr.com, www.pslab.net

Photos
Diane Aftimos

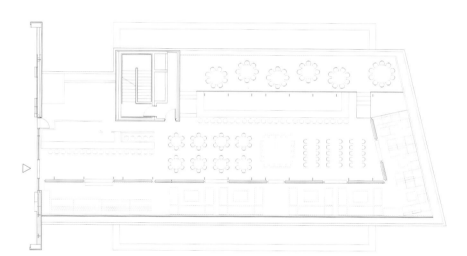

One of the coolest lounge restaurants in Beirut has taken up residence in the middle of the city on the roof of the An-Nahar high rise. Guests dine al fresco, soaking up the Mediterranean ambience, or enjoy the panoramic views while sipping a drink at the bar. Late in the evening, Iris becomes a lounge featuring live music or DJs. The menu offers a variety of grilled fish and seafood along with a range of sushi offerings to go with cocktails sporting names like "Pornstar Martini" and "Tommy's Margarita." During the day, urban Beirut with its harbor forms the backdrop; after sundown, a lighting concept by .PSLAB featuring customized lights provides a fitting atmosphere. Black steel V-shaped lighting fixtures suspended by steel cables float over the bar where countless light bulbs bathe the area in light. The city's young, hip crowd gathers at Iris on warm summer nights.

Auf dem Dach des An-Nahar-Hochhauses mitten im Zentrum von Beirut hat eines der angesagtesten Lounge-Restaurants der Stadt seinen Platz gefunden. Unter freiem Himmel diniert man in mediterranem Ambiente oder genießt beim Drink an der Bar die Panorama-Aussicht, bevor das Iris zu später Stunde zur Lounge mit Live-Musik oder DJ-Sounds wird. Zum „Pornstar Martini" oder „Tommy's Margarita" hält die Speisekarte eine Auswahl an Fisch und Meeresfrüchten vom Grill oder in Form von Sushi und Co. bereit. Tagsüber bildet das urbane Beirut mit seinem Hafen die Kulisse, nach Sonnenuntergang sorgt das Lichtkonzept von .PSLAB mit eigens angefertigten Leuchten für die passende Atmosphäre. Von Stahlseilen gehalten schweben schwarze Stahlträger über der Bar, deren unzählige Birnen warmes Licht verströmen. In lauen Sommernächten versammelt sich im Iris das junge Szenevolk der Stadt.

L'un des lounge-restaurants les plus prisés de Beyrouth se trouve sur le toit de l'immeuble An-Nahar, en plein centre-ville. À ciel ouvert, vous pouvez dîner dans une ambiance méditerranéenne ou profiter du panorama depuis le bar, un verre à la main. En fin de soirée, l'Iris se transforme en lounge d'où résonne la musique de concerts ou de DJs. Outre les cocktails tels que le « Pornstar Martini » ou le « Tommy's Margarita », le menu propose poissons et fruits de mer grillés ou en sushis. La journée, l'animation de Beyrouth et de son port se suffit à elle-même, mais après le coucher du soleil, l'aménagement lumineux de .PSLAB, fait sur mesure, entre en jeu. Au-dessus du bar, d'innombrables ampoules pendent à de longues poutrelles en acier noir diffusent ainsi une lumière chaude, autour de laquelle la jeunesse de la ville aime se retrouver lors des douces nuits d'été.

Momo at the Souks

Beirut, Lebanon

Beirut Souks, Jewelery Souk 7
Beirut, 01-972808

Phone: +961 1 999 767
www.momobeirut.com

Prices: $$$
Cuisine: Oriental-French

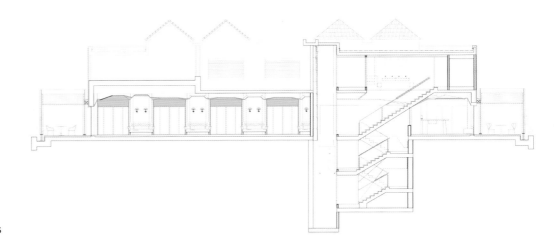

Architecture/Design
Annabel Karim Kassar
www.annabelkassar.com

Photos
Ray Main
courtesy of Annabel Karim Kassar & Associés

Well-known primarily through his London restaurant Momo, restaurateur Mourad Mazouz had already worked with architect Annabel Karim Kassar on Almaz by Momo, his branch in Dubai. During the construction of Mazouz' latest offshoot in Beirut, Kassar and her team transformed the four floors of a former office building into a 13,200-square-foot café restaurant. Momo at the Souks has two kitchens, a bar, two lounges featuring abundant greenery, and a spacious terrace. The interior reflects the colorful hustle and bustle of a souk and feels like an ultramodern patchwork: Covering the entire interior space, a three-dimensional ceiling design using geometric shapes contrasts with the simple cast floor and the ornamental decor of wallpapers, cushions, and carpets. The menu features modern Lebanese dishes and some classics from Momo.

Der vor allem durch sein Londoner Restaurant Momo bekannt gewordene Gastronom Mourad Mazouz hat bereits bei seiner Dependance in Dubai, Almaz by Momo, mit Architektin Annabel Karim Kassar zusammengearbeitet. Bei der Realisierung des jüngsten Ablegers in Beirut haben Kassar und ihr Team die vier Stockwerke eines ehemaligen Bürogebäudes in ein 1 226 Quadratmeter großes Café-Restaurant verwandelt. Hier finden zwei Küchen Platz, eine Bar, begrünte Lounges und eine großzügige Terrasse. Das Interieur greift das bunte Treiben der Souks auf und wirkt wie ein hochmodernes Patchwork: Eine dreidimensionale Deckenkonstruktion aus geometrischen Formen, die den gesamten Innenraum überspannt, kontrastiert mit dem einfachen Gussboden sowie dem ornamentalen Dekor von Wandtapete, Polstern und Teppichen. Auf der Speisekarte stehen moderne libanesische Gerichte und einige von Momos Klassikern.

Le gastronome Mourad Mazouz est devenu célèbre grâce à son restaurant londonien, Momo. Il a décidé de confier la réalisation de son antenne de Beyrouth à l'architecte Annabel Karim Kassar, avec laquelle il a déjà travaillé à Dubaï pour son enseigne Almaz by Momo. Kassar et son équipe ont ainsi transformé un bâtiment de quatre étages, qui abritait des bureaux, en un café-restaurant de 1 226 mètres carrés composé notamment de deux cuisines, un bar, des salons lounge verdoyants et une large terrasse. L'intérieur s'inspire de l'atmosphère multicolore des souks et ressemble à un patchwork ultra-moderne : un plafond en trois dimensions, tout en formes géométriques, recouvre l'intérieur et contraste avec le sol en simple béton coulé et le décor ornemental fait de tapisseries murales, de coussins et de tapis. Le menu propose des plats libanais modernes ainsi que certains des classiques de Momo.

Konoba

Mahé, Seychelles

Angel Fish Bayside Marina, Roche Caiman
Mahé

Phone: +248 4345 400
www.konoba.sc

Prices: $$
Cuisine: International

Architecture/Design
Albert Angel
www.albert-angel.com

Photos
Dušan Kochol

A school of over 7,000 metal fish wend their way throughout the interior as if following an invisible current. Illuminated by blue light, the design creates the illusion of an underwater world such as the coral reefs of the Seychelles. The limited color palette is a maritime combination of white and blue, a perfect choice against the backdrop of the yacht harbor and the view of Eden Island. Dedon armchairs on the terrace offer an inviting place to relax in the shade of umbrellas. The menu offers a wide variety of fish and seafood from the Indian Ocean, complemented by a selection of international wines from the restaurant's own wine cellar which comprises over 2,000 bottles. Konoba features live music three evenings a week. Guests can dance in the bar area illuminated by the fish installation, for which Albert Angel was shortlisted for the famous Restaurant & Bar Design Award.

Als würde er einer unsichtbaren Strömung folgen, zieht sich ein Schwarm von über 7 000 Metallfischen durch den gesamten Innenraum. Von blauem Licht angestrahlt entsteht die Illusion einer Unterwasserwelt wie in den Korallenriffen der Seychellen. Passend zur Kulisse des Yachthafens und dem Blick auf Eden Island beschränkt sich die Farbpalette auf eine maritime Kombination aus Weiß und Blau. Dedon-Sessel auf der Terrasse laden ein, im Schatten der Sonnenschirme zu relaxen. Die Speisekarte offeriert alle Arten von Fisch und Meeresfrüchten aus dem Indischen Ozean, begleitet von einer Auswahl an internationalen Weinen aus dem hauseigenen Vorrat von über 2 000 Flaschen. An drei Abenden der Woche gibt es im Konoba Live-Musik. Getanzt wird im Bar-Bereich im Schein der Fischinstallation, für die Albert Angel für den renommierten Restaurant & Bar Design Award nominiert war.

Un banc de plus de 7 000 poissons métalliques se fraye un chemin à travers la salle, suivant un courant invisible. L'éclairage bleu donne l'illusion d'un monde sous-marin semblable à celui de la barrière de corail des Seychelles. En harmonie avec le port de plaisance et la vue sur Eden Island, la palette de couleurs se limite à une combinaison maritime de bleu et de blanc. Sur la terrasse, des fauteuils Dedon invitent à la détente à l'ombre des parasols. Le menu propose toutes sortes de poissons et de fruits de mers de l'Océan Indien, ainsi qu'une sélection de vins du monde entier, issus de la cave du restaurant où sont conservées plus de 2 000 bouteilles. Le Konoba propose en outre des concerts trois soirs par semaine. L'espace bar permet de danser sous le scintillement des poissons, pour lesquels Albert Angel a été nominé pour le célèbre Restaurant & Bar Design Award.

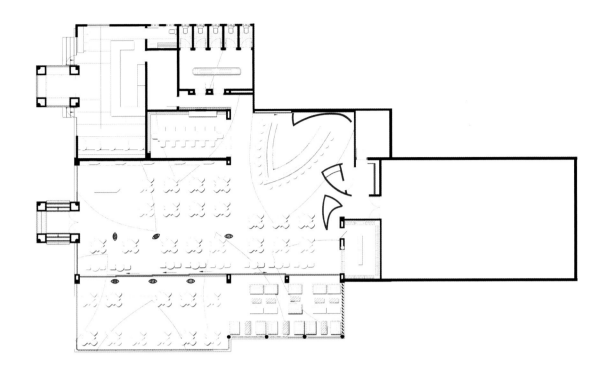

Makaron

Stellenbosch, South Africa

26–32, Houtkapper Street
Stellenbosch, 7600

Phone: +27 21 880 1549
www.makaronrestaurant.co.za

Prices: $$$
Cuisine: Molecular

Architecture/Design
Etienne Hanekom
www.visi.co.za

Photos
courtesy of Majeka House

In 2011, interior designer Etienne Hanekom gave a new look to Majeka House, a five-star resort in the vineyards east of Cape Town. Makaron restaurant also shows the signature touch of the art director of VISI, a South African design magazine. Chef Tanja Kruger serves French-inspired dishes. The restaurant's center-piece is a buffet with 18 identical lamps; although they are actually ordinary aluminum lamps, Hanekom had their metal surface anodized, and as a result they now shimmer in a lovely shade of golden bronze. Philippe Starck's transparent plastic Ghost Chairs from Kartell are paired with dark wood tables and baroque chairs on a herringbone parquet floor. In the Cigar Lounge, leather armchairs create a dignified atmosphere in front of the fireplace.

Interior Designer Etienne Hanekom hat dem Fünf-Sterne-Resort Majeka House in den Weinbergen östlich von Kapstadt 2011 einen neuen Look verpasst. Auch das Restaurant Makaron trägt die Handschrift des Art Directors von VISI, einem südafrikanischen Design-Magazin. Küchenchefin Tanja Kruger serviert hier ihre französisch inspirierten Gerichte. Herzstück ist das Buffet mit 18 gleichartigen Leuchten. Eigentlich handelte es sich um gewöhnliche Aluminium-Lampen, deren Metalloberfläche Hanekom jedoch eloxieren ließ. So schimmern die Schirme jetzt in einem Gold-Bronze-Ton. Auf dem edlen Fischgrätparkett wurden Philippe Starcks Ghost Chairs von Kartell in transparentem Kunststoff zu dunklen Holztischen und barocken Stühlen kombiniert. In der Cigar Lounge sorgen mit Leder bezogene Sessel für eine gediegene Atmosphäre vor dem Kamin.

Le designer d'intérieur Etienne Hanekom a relooké en 2011 l'hôtel cinq étoiles Majeka House, situé dans les vignobles à l'est du Cap. Le restaurant Makaron n'a pas non plus échappé à la griffe du directeur artistique du magazine sud-africain VISI, spécialisé dans le design. La chef Tanja Kruger propose des plats inspirés des saveurs françaises. Le joyau du lieu est son buffet illuminé de 18 lampes similaires. Il s'agit en fait de lampes traditionnelles en aluminium, dont Hanekom a anodisé la surface métallique pour leur donner un reflet or-bronze. L'élégant parquet en arrête de poisson et les chaises Ghost en plastique transparent, conçues pour Kartell par Philippe Starck, s'allient aux tables de bois foncé et chaises baroques pour parfaire le nouveau look de l'ensemble. Le Cigar Lounge avec ses fauteuils de cuir invite à la détente devant la cheminée.

Cape to Cuba

Cape Town, South Africa

165 Main Road, Kalk Bay
Cape Town, 7990

Phone: +27 21 788 1566
www.kalkbaycapetocuba.com

Prices: $$
Cuisine: Seafood Grill

Architecture/Design
Bartel van Vuuren
www.sobeitstudio.com

Photos
Simon Scarboro

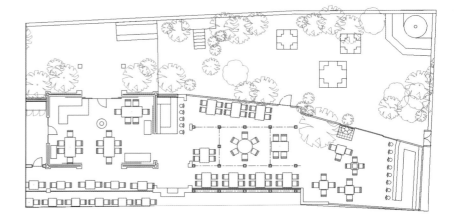

You could almost believe that the hut on the beach of Kalk Bay, South Africa, is the hideout of a devout Cuban pirate and part-time poet, stranded in this fishing village on the Cape of Good Hope. The restaurant's decor consists of an impressive hodgepodge of chandeliers, devotional objects, vases, and references to Ernest Hemingway and Che Guevara, the inspiration behind the name of the restaurant's bar. Classic cocktails such as mojitos, Bloody Marys, and daiquiris are listed at the top of the menu in memory of the revolutionary from Cuba and the famous author and his love of the Caribbean and strong liquor. The restaurant features authentic Cuban dishes with Cajun influences as well as punches of heat supplied by chilies. After dessert, you can dream of nights in far-off Havana while savoring the taste of a cigar.

Fast könnte man meinen, die Hütte am Strand des südafrikanischen Ortes Kalk Bay sei das Versteck eines strenggläubigen, kubanischen Piraten und Teilzeit-Poeten, den es in das Fischerdorf am Kap der Guten Hoffnung verschlagen hat. Die Einrichtung des Restaurants ist ein beeindruckendes Sammelsurium von Kronleuchtern, Devotionalien, Vasen und Erinnerungen an Ernest Hemingway und Che Guevara, den Namensgeber der hauseigenen Bar. In Gedenken an den Revolutionär aus Kuba und den bekannten Schriftsteller mit seiner Liebe für die Karibikinsel und Hochprozentiges stehen Cocktailklassiker wie Mojito, Bloody Mary und Daiquiri ganz oben auf der Karte. Serviert werden authentische kubanische Gerichte mit Einflüssen der Cajun-Küche und der Schärfe von Chilis. Nach dem Dessert lässt sich beim Geschmack einer Zigarre von Nächten im fernen Havanna träumen.

Cette cabane sur la plage de Kalk Bay, en Afrique du Sud, pourrait presque être le repaire d'un pirate cubain très croyant et poète à ses heures perdues, arrivé par hasard dans ce petit village de pêcheurs du Cap de Bonne-Espérance. La décoration du restaurant est un impressionnant capharnaüm de lustres, objets religieux, vase et souvenirs à la gloire d'Ernest Hemingway et Che Guevara, dont le bar porte par ailleurs le nom. En mémoire du révolutionnaire de Cuba et du célèbre écrivain, amoureux de cette île des Caraïbes et amateur de rhum, le menu propose bien évidemment des cocktails tels que le mojito, le bloody mary ou le daïquiri. Vous retrouverez également d'authentiques plats cubains, influencés par la cuisine cajun et agrémentés de piments rouges. Après le dessert, laissez-vous emporter par le rêve de nuits à La Havane, un cigare aux lèvres.

At.mosphere

Dubai, United Arab Emirates

at Burj Khalifa, 1 Emaar Boulevard
Dubai

Phone: +971 4 888 3828
www.atmosphereburjkhalifa.com

Prices: $$$$
Cuisine: Grill

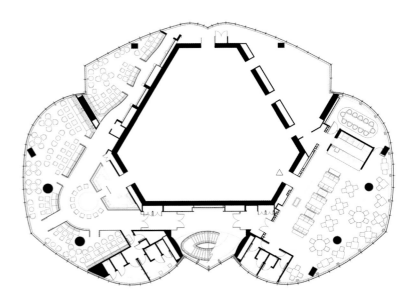

Architecture/Design
Adam D. Tihany
www.tihanydesign.com

Photos
Eric Laignel

Exactly one minute is how long the express elevator takes to travel 122 floors. Located at an elevation of 1,450 feet in Burj Khalifa, the world's tallest building, the restaurant and lounge offer breathtaking views of Dubai and the Persian Gulf. Adam D. Tihany designed the interior, using polished mahogany and earth-toned textiles throughout, including the private dining room seating up to twelve people. Whether stopping by the lounge for a drink or allowing Michelin star chef Dwayne Cheer to spoil your taste buds in The Grill restaurant, here even the restrooms with views of the Emirates are an experience. As the highest restaurant in the world, At.mosphere holds an entry in the Guinness Book of World Records. It's no surprise that in these surroundings, high tea—a tea break in the afternoon popular in Arab culture—takes on an entirely new meaning.

Exakt eine Minute braucht der Expressaufzug für 122 Stockwerke. Auf Höhenmeter 442 des Burj Khalifa, des höchsten Gebäudes der Erde, befinden sich Restaurant und Lounge mit einem atemberaubenden Ausblick über Dubai und den persischen Golf. Adam D. Tihany gestaltete die Räumlichkeiten in poliertem Mahagoni und erdfarbenen Textilien, darunter auch einen Private Dining Room für bis zu zwölf Personen. Ganz gleich, ob man für einen Drink in der Lounge einkehrt oder sich im Grillrestaurant von Sternekoch Dwayne Cheer verwöhnen lässt – hier wird sogar der Gang zur Toilette mit Blick über das Emirat zum Erlebnis. Als höchstes Restaurant der Welt hat das At.mosphere einen Eintrag ins Guinnessbuch der Rekorde erhalten, und so bekommt der High Tea, die bei den Arabern beliebte Teepause am Nachmittag, in dieser Umgebung eine ganz neue Bedeutung.

L'ascenseur a besoin d'exactement une minute pour gravir les 122 étages. Le restaurant et le lounge se trouvent à 422 mètres de hauteur, perché sur la plus haute tour du monde, la Burj Khalifa. La vue sur Dubaï et le golfe persique y est à couper le souffle. Les lieux ont été aménagés par Adam D. Tihany à l'aide d'acajou poli et de textiles aux couleurs ocres ; la salle à manger privée peut accueillir jusqu'à douze personnes et le trajet jusqu'aux toilettes est également une expérience extraordinaire où vous pouvez admirer l'ensemble de l'émirat. Vous pouvez boire un verre dans le lounge ou bien déguster les grillades du chef étoilé Dwayne Cheer. Le Guinness des Records mentionne l'At.mosphere comme étant le plus haut restaurant du monde, et le « High Tea », la pause thé du milieu d'après-midi, si prisée de la population locale, prend en ces lieux une toute autre dimension.

Empório Baglioni

São Paulo, Brasil

Rua Pedroso Alvarenga, 708
São Paulo, 04531-002

Phone: +55 11 3167 0388

Prices: $$
Cuisine: Deli

Architecture/Design
Rocco, Vidal +arquitetos
www.roccovidal.com.br

Photos
courtesy of Rocco, Vidal +arquitetos

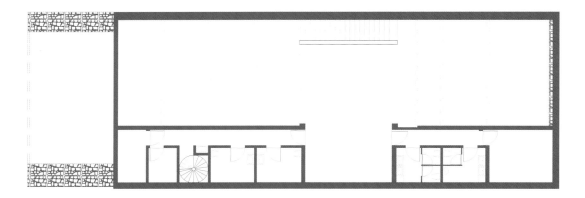

From the outside, the Empório Baglioni seems ordinary. You would never guess that a cathedral-like space opens up behind its doors, which are shielded by chain net latticework. A mezzanine floor extends through roughly half of the space. Both levels feature gray tables and chairs whose color matches the exposed concrete of the suspended ceiling and the rough stone walls. These striking walls are continued on the exterior façade. Wood paneling on the interior walls provide a warm contrast to the stone and concrete. Angled skylights bathe the room in natural light, which accentuates the large black and white photographs. The team of Rocco, Vidal +arquitetos handled the restaurant design. This architectural and planning office from São Paulo has been designing private homes and public buildings for more than 30 years.

Von außen sieht das Baglioni unscheinbar aus. Niemals würde man vermuten, dass sich hinter den Türen, die mit einem Kettennetz vergittert sind, ein kathedralenartig hoher Raum auftut. Etwa zur Hälfte ist er durch ein Zwischengeschoss unterteilt. Oben und unten stehen graue Tische und Stühle. Sie sind im gleichen Ton wie der Sichtbeton der Zwischendecke und die rohen Steinmauern gehalten. Die markanten Mauern finden sich auch an der Außenfassade wieder. Einen warmen Kontrast bilden Holzvertäfelungen an den Wänden. Schräge Dachfenster lassen natürliches Licht in den Raum, das die großen Schwarz-Weiß-Fotografien hervorhebt. Der Entwurf des Restaurants stammt von Rocco, Vidal und ihrem Team. Das Architektur- und Planungsbüro aus São Paulo gestaltet seit mehr als 30 Jahren Privathäuser und öffentliche Gebäude.

De l'extérieur, le Baglioni ne paye pas de mine. Il serait même inimaginable que ces portes grillagées puissent ouvrir sur une salle aux allures de cathédrale, séparée en son milieu d'un entresol. La couleur grise des tables et des chaises est en harmonie avec les tons du béton apparent du plafond de l'entresol, ainsi qu'avec les murs de briques brutes que l'on retrouve également sur la façade extérieure. L'ensemble est agréablement contrasté par les boiseries murales. Des fenêtres inclinées laissent filtrer la lumière du jour, qui vient mettre en valeur les grandes photographies noir et blanc. Cet assemblage artistique est l'œuvre de Rocco, Vidal et leur équipe. Ce bureau d'études et d'architecte de São Paulo collectionne les projets d'aménagement de maisons privées et bâtiments publics depuis 30 ans.

Hawksworth Restaurant

Vancouver, Canada

801 West Georgia Street
Vancouver, V6P 1C7

Phone: +1 604 673 7000
www.hawksworthrestaurant.com

Prices: $$$
Cuisine: Canadian

Architecture/Design
Munge Leung
www.mungeleung.com

Photos
Martin Tessler
courtesy of Munge Leung

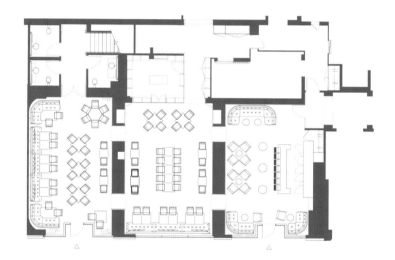

Visitors are captivated by the wealth of detail in the furnishings and cuisine of Hawksworth Restaurant in the Rosewood Hotel Georgia. Chef David Hawksworth, who perfected his craft in Michelin star restaurants in France and Great Britain, was named Vancouver's Chef of the Year in 2012. In his creations, he fuses various national cuisines and is committed to using high-quality seasonal ingredients. Munge Leung designed the restaurant's three rooms to complement its setting within the historic Hotel: In the bar lounge, a glowing ceiling floats above the leather-clad bar; an impressive crystal chandelier illuminates the Pearl Room with its wall relief; and an art installation by Rodney Graham adorns the walls of the Art Room. Subdued lighting and two gas fireplaces convey a cozy atmosphere, and even the cooled wine room fits in harmoniously with the overall concept.

Sowohl die Einrichtung als auch die Küche des Hawksworth Restaurants im Rosewood Hotel Georgia bestechen durch ihren Facettenreichtum. Küchenchef David Hawksworth, der sein Handwerk in französischen und britischen Sternerestaurants perfektioniert hat, wurde 2012 Vancouvers Koch des Jahres. In seinen Kreationen verbindet er verschiedene Landesküchen und richtet sich stets nach saisonalem Angebot und Qualität der Ware. Dem Rahmen des historischen Hotels entsprechend gestalteten Munge Leung die drei Räume des Restaurants: In der Bar-Lounge schwebt eine leuchtende Decke über dem lederbeschlagenen Tresen, ein imposanter Kristalllüster erhellt den Pearl Room mit seinem Wandrelief, und die Wände des Art Room ziert eine Kunstinstallation von Rodney Graham. Gedimmtes Licht und zwei Gaskamine vermitteln Wohnlichkeit, und auch der Weinkühlschrank fügt sich in das stimmige Gesamtbild ein.

La décoration et la cuisine du Hawksworth Restaurant, au Rosewood Hotel Georgia, fascinent toutes deux par leurs multiples facettes. Le chef David Hawksworth, formé dans des restaurants étoilés de France et d'Angleterre, a été élu cuisinier de l'année à Vancouver en 2012. Ses créations allient des spécialités de différents pays et il porte une grande attention aux offres saisonnières ainsi qu'à la qualité des produits. Trois salles ont été décorées en accord avec le cadre environnant de l'hôtel historique par Munge Leung : un plafond lumineux éclaire ainsi le comptoir recouvert de cuir du bar-lounge, un lustre en cristal illumine la Pearl Room et ses reliefs muraux, et les murs de l'Art Room sont ornés d'une installation artistique de Rodney Graham. Une lumière tamisée et deux cheminées au gaz apportent une touche de confort à l'ensemble, auquel l'armoire frigorifique à vin s'intègre joliment.

Tori Tori

Mexico City, Mexico

Temístocles 61
Mexico City, 11560

Phone: +52 55 5281 8112
www.toritori.com.mx

Prices: $$
Cuisine: Japanese

Architecture/Design
Rojkind Arquitectos & ESRAWE Studio
www.rojkindarquitectos.com, www.esrawe.com

Photos
Paul Rivera/archphoto

The architecture of this building comes across like a futuristic vision. A lattice structure of milled steel conceals a Japanese restaurant featuring a highly unusual design. Architects from Rojkind Arquitectos and Esrawe Studio collaborated on the design of the building and its rooms as well as on all the furniture for the interior and exterior areas. The core of the interior is the tea room with low Zataku tables positioned over recessed floor openings and a vertical garden illuminated from above by a large skylight. On warm evenings, guests can dine on the terrace surrounded by lush greenery and the blue glow from the façade. At Tori Tori, you can enjoy the full spectrum of Japanese cuisine—soups, teriyakis, noodles, curries, tempuras, sushi, and sashimi—in a variety probably rarely seen outside of Japan.

Wie eine Zukunftsvision wirkt die Architektur des Gebäudes. Hinter der Gitterstruktur aus gefrästem Stahl verbirgt sich ein japanisches Restaurant mit außergewöhnlichem Design. In einer Kooperation haben die Architekten von Rojkind Arquitectos und Esrawe Studio nicht nur das Gebäude und dessen Räume gestaltet, sondern auch sämtliches Mobiliar für Innen- und Außenbereich. Herzstück des Interieurs ist der Tea Room mit in den Boden eingelassenen Zataku-Sitztischen und einem vertikalen Garten, der von einem Oberlicht erhellt wird. An lauen Abenden kann man, umgeben von üppigem Grün, im blauen Schein der Fassade auf der Terrasse dinieren. Im Tori Tori zeigt sich das gesamte Spektrum japanischer Kochkunst: Suppen, Teriyakis, Nudeln, Currys, Tempuras, Sushi und Sashimi, die man in einer ähnlichen Vielfalt wahrscheinlich selten außerhalb Japans erhält.

L'architecture du bâtiment est des plus futuristes, et ce qui se cache sous ce gigantesque filet en acier est un restaurant japonais au design extraordinaire. Les architectes de Rojkind Arquitectos et d'Esrawe Studio ont travaillé de concert sur la conception de l'édifice et de ses pièces, mais aussi sur le choix de l'ensemble du mobilier des espaces intérieur et extérieur. Le salon de thé vaut particulièrement le détour, avec ses tables basses Zataku fixées dans le sol et son jardin vertical éclairé d'en haut. Lorsque le temps le permet, vous pouvez dîner sur la terrasse, au milieu de plantes luxuriantes, sous la lumière bleue de la façade. Le Tori Tori propose toute la gamme culinaire japonaise : soupe, teriyaki, nouilles, curry, tempura, sushi et sashimi. La variété des plats est telle qu'elle ne se retrouve probablement qu'au Japon.

Beijing Noodle No. 9

Las Vegas, USA

at Caesars Palace, 3570 Las Vegas Boulevard South
Las Vegas, NV 89109

Phone: +1 877 346 4642
www.caesarspalace.com

Prices: $$
Cuisine: Chinese

Architecture/Design
design spirits co., ltd.
www.design-spirits.com

Photos
Barry Johnson

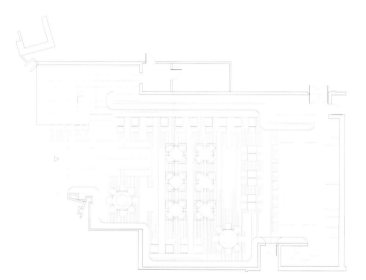

As a "white cube," the restaurant offers a refreshing change of pace to the dark gaming areas, patterned carpets, and colorful flashing lights of the slot machines at Caesars Palace Casino. The architecture by Design Spirits has largely done away with colors, choosing to instead focus on the interplay of light and shadows. Like an enormous silhouette, the white metal ceiling hovers over the room and sleekly extends down to form the interior walls. Goldfish aquariums act as partitions and add colorful accents that are repeated in splashes of color on the water glasses. A spice rack over the open show kitchen adds another vivid eye-catching accent. As promised by the name, hand-made Chinese noodles are the specialty of the house; however, Chef Li Yu also prepares Asian soups, dim sum, and fresh seafood in true Asian style.

Als „white cube" bietet das Restaurant eine erfrischende Abwechslung zu den dunklen Spielhallen, gemusterten Teppichen und bunten Blinklichtern der Automaten im Caesars Palace Casino. Die Architektur von Design Spirits verzichtet weitestgehend auf Farben und konzentriert sich auf das Spiel von Licht und Schatten. Wie ein enormer Scherenschnitt legt sich die weiße Metalldecke über den Raum und formt dabei gleichzeitig die Innenwände, während Goldfischaquarien Raumaufteilung und Farbakzente bringen, die sich in den getupften Wassergläsern wiederfinden. Einen weiteren bunten Blickfang bietet ein Gewürzregal über der offenen Showküche. Wie der Name verspricht, sind handgemachte, chinesiche Nudeln die Spezialität des Hauses; aber auch asiatische Suppen, Dim Sum und frische Meeresfrüchte werden von Küchenchef Li Yu nach bester Manier zubereitet.

Ce « cube blanc » offre une alternative rafraîchissante aux salles de jeux sombres, aux tapis opulents et aux lumières multicolores des automates du Caesars Palace Casino. L'architecture de Design Spirits renonce largement aux couleurs pour se concentrer sur les jeux d'ombre et de lumière. Le plafond métallique blanc s'étend comme une énorme silhouette au-dessus des têtes et se prolonge jusque sur les murs intérieurs. Des aquariums de poissons rouges viennent partager la pièce et apporter des accents colorés que l'on retrouve dans les verres mouchetés. Une étagère à épices située au-dessus de la cuisine ouverte offre une autre touche de couleur. Ainsi que son nom l'indique, les nouilles chinoises, faites à la main, sont la spécialité du chef Li Yu, qui prépare également avec plaisir des soupes asiatiques, du dimsum et des fruits de mer frais.

Delphine

Los Angeles, USA

6250 Hollywood Boulevard
Los Angeles, CA 90028

Phone: +1 323 798 1355
www.restaurantdelphine.com

Prices: $$
Cuisine: Californian

Architecture/Design
MARKZEFF
www.markzeff.com

Photos
Todd Vitti Photography (3)
Skott Snider (1)

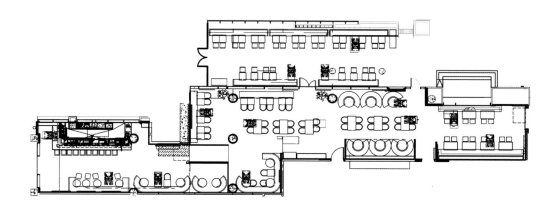

For New York interior designer Mark Zeff, the ocean and the beach were the key inspirations behind the interior design for Delphine. After all, the menu for this restaurant located in the heart of Hollywood features primarily seafood. Bistro tables combined with a white and blue tile floor introduce a hint of the Riviera. Oversized oval mirrors with wide wooden frames are mounted on the walls and reflect the light. The walls feature black and white photographs with beach motifs, a detail reminiscent of the 1920s and '30s. Built-in illuminated bookcases give the interior the feeling of a living room. The ceiling of the spacious room is clad in wooden slats and extends in arches supported by pillars of exposed concrete.

Das Meer und der Strand waren für den New Yorker Interior Designer Mark Zeff die wichtigste Inspiration beim Gestalten der Inneneinrichtung des Delphine. Schließlich serviert das Restaurant im Herzen Hollywoods vor allem Seafood. Ein Hauch von Riviera schwingt mit, wenn Bistrotische zu einem weiß-blauen Kachelboden kombiniert werden. Überdimensionale, ovale Spiegel mit breiten Holzrahmen an den Wänden reflektieren das Licht. Eine Reminiszenz an die 20er und 30er Jahre sind die Schwarz-Weiß-Fotografien mit Strand-Motiven an den Wänden. Ein illuminiertes Wandregal verbreitet Wohnzimmeratmosphäre. Die Decke des großzügigen Raumes ist mit Holzleisten ausgekleidet. Sie verläuft in Bögen, die von Säulen aus Sichtbeton getragen werden.

Pour l'aménagement du Delphine, le designer d'intérieur new-yorkais Mark Zeff s'est laissé inspirer par le bleu de la mer et les plages de sable chaud. Cela constitue un cadre parfait pour ce restaurant situé dans le cœur du quartier d'Hollywood, dont la carte propose essentiellement poissons et fruits de mer. L'ensemble est agrémenté d'une ambiance Riviera avec des tables de bistrot sur un sol de faïence bleu et blanc. Les miroirs surdimensionnés et ovales dans des cadres de bois reflètent la lumière. Celle-ci illumine ainsi les photographies noir et blanc aux motifs de plage qui rappellent les années 20 et 30. Une étagère murale éclairée parfait cette atmosphère de salon. Les boiseries du plafond se perdent en courbes jusqu'au sommet des colonnes en béton apparent.

STK Midtown

New York, USA

Grace Building, 1114 Avenue of the Americas
New York City, NY 10036

Phone: +1 646 624 2455
www.stkhouse.com

Prices: $$$
Cuisine: Steakhouse

Architecture/Design
ICRAVE
www.icrave.com

Photos
courtesy of ICRAVE

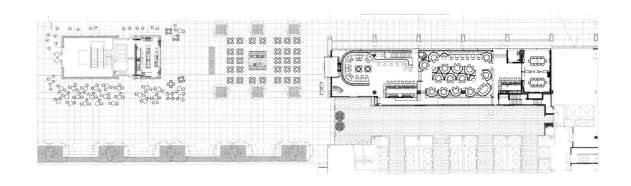

Behind the curved façade of the Grace Building is the second New York branch of this popular steak house concept, with branches now open in four American cities. Drawing inspiration from the dynamics of the building, designers from ICRAVE created a rib-like structure supported by columns that echo the shape of a wave. Trademarks of STK restaurants are semi-circular banquettes upholstered in leather, high-gloss wooden tables, and chairs with crossing legs. The steaks are grilled to perfection and served with homemade sauces and refined side dishes, including parmesan truffle fries and American classics like mac & cheese. Desserts, including a molten chocolate cake or a refreshing sorbet, are a perfect way to wind up dinner. In the summer, the terrace with a separate bar is an inviting place to relax in the shade of the Midtown skyscrapers.

Hinter der geschwungenen Fassade des Grace Building befindet sich die zweite New Yorker Filiale des beliebten Steakhauskonzeptes, das mittlerweile in vier amerikanischen Metropolen zuhause ist. In Anlehnung an die Dynamik des Gebäudes entwarfen die Designer von ICRAVE eine auf Säulen stehende Rippenstruktur, welche die Form einer Welle nachzeichnet. Markenzeichen der STK-Restaurants sind halbrunde, ledergepolsterte Sitzbänke, hochglänzende Holztische und Stühle mit sich überkreuzenden Beinen. Die Steaks sind auf den Punkt gegrillt, dazu werden hausgemachte Saucen und raffinierte Beilagen serviert, darunter „parmesan truffle fries" oder amerikanische Klassiker wie „mac & cheese". Desserts wie der „molten chocolate cake" oder ein erfrischendes Sorbet runden das Dinner ab. Im Sommer lädt die Terrasse mit eigener Bar zum Relaxen im Schatten der Wolkenkratzer von Midtown.

La deuxième filiale new-yorkaise de la célèbre chaîne de restaurants à viande, présente dans quatre métropoles américaines, se trouve derrière la façade arquée du Grace Building. Se servant de la dynamique du bâtiment, les designers d'ICRAVE ont imaginé une structure en forme de côtes, qui repose sur des piliers et forme une vague. Les marques de fabrique des restaurants STK ne sont pas en reste : bancs en cuir semi-ronds, tables en bois brillantes et chaises aux pattes entrecroisées. Les steaks sont grillés à point et servis avec des sauces faites maison et des accompagnements raffinés, tels que des « parmesan truffle fries » ou des classiques américains comme le « mac & cheese ». Les desserts tels que le « molten chocolate cake » ou les sorbets rafraîchissants sont également succulents. L'été, la terrasse et son bar invitent à la détente, à l'ombre des gratte-ciel de Midtown.

abc kitchen

New York, USA

35 E 18th Street
New York City, NY 10003

Phone: +1 212 475 5829
www.abckitchennyc.com

Prices: $$$
Cuisine: American-International

Architecture/Design
abc carpet & home
www.abchome.com

Photos
Claudia Hehr

The ABC team is committed to regional, ecological, and sustainable creations—and not just in the cuisine of chef Daniel Kluger. Even the interior furnishings reflect a connection to nature and come from the immediate vicinity. Artist and furniture designer Eric Slayton, who lives in Brooklyn, designed the bar. The overall design was the product of the ABC Home Creative Team, which operates one of its large furnishing stores in the same building. Guests dine under filigree chandeliers, sleek industrial lighting, and naked light bulbs. White chairs contrast with different types of wood. Tables constructed of oversized tree planks and supported by metal frames are particularly striking. The flooring is wood as well. Nature photography hangs on the white-painted brick walls.

Das ABC-Team setzt auf regionale, ökologische und nachhaltige Kreationen – und das nicht nur beim Essen von Chefkoch Daniel Kluger. Auch die Inneneinrichtung soll Naturverbundenheit ausdrücken und kommt aus der näheren Umgebung. So hat der Künstler und Möbeldesigner Eric Slayton aus Brooklyn die Bar gestaltet. Der Gesamtentwurf ist vom ABC Home Creative Team, das im gleichen Haus eines seiner großen Einrichtungsgeschäfte betreibt. Man tafelt unter filigranen Kronleuchtern, schlichten Industrieleuchten und nackten Glühbirnen. Zu dem Weiß der Stühle gesellen sich verschiedene Holzarten. Bemerkenswert sind die Tische mit Platten aus überdimensionalen Baumscheiben, die von Metallgestellen getragen werden. Auch der Boden ist aus Holz. An den weißgestrichenen Backsteinwänden hängen Naturfotografien.

L'équipe d'ABC a choisi de s'inspirer de la nature pour la décoration intérieure qui se reflète dans les créations régionales, écologiques et durables. Ce concept se retrouve également dans les mets du chef Daniel Kluger. Le bar a été conçu par l'artiste et designer de meubles Eric Slayton, originaire de Brooklyn, tandis que l'ensemble est une œuvre d'ABC Home Creative Team, dont la boutique de décoration d'intérieur se situe dans le même bâtiment. On se restaure sous des lustres en filigrane, des lampes industrielles et des ampoules nues. Le blanc des chaises s'accorde parfaitement avec la variété des bois utilisés, et les tables formées de plaques de troncs d'arbres surdimensionnées montées sur des socles en métal ne manquent pas d'attirer le regard. Trônant au-dessus du sol également en bois, des photographies de paysages naturels sont accrochées aux murs de briques peintes en blanc.

Delicatessen

New York, USA

54 Prince Street
New York City, NY 10012

Phone: +1 212 226 0211
www.delicatessennyc.com

Prices: $$
Cuisine: American Bistro

Architecture/Design
nemaworkshop
www.nemaworkshop.com

Photos
David Joseph

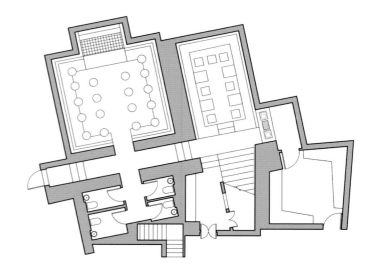

Between the Manhattan neighborhoods of SoHo and NoLIta, this restaurant is a favorite primarily because of its no-frills cuisine and relaxed atmosphere. Chef Michael Ferraro describes the popular classics with a pinch of innovation on his menu as "international comfort food." His version of a perfect place for a quick snack has paved the way for a new generation of American delicatessens, delis for short. The nemaworkshop architectural team came up with the concept of a loft-like location featuring a stainless steel façade and steel-and-glass garage doors that can be opened completely, erasing the boundaries between indoors and out. On the lower level, a padded lounge with a glass roof and a wall mural by artist Juan José Heredia has a bar that offers drinks in the evening.

Das Restaurant zwischen Manhattans Stadtvierteln SoHo und NoLIta ist vor allem wegen seiner schnörkellosen Küche und der entspannten Atmosphäre beliebt. Als International Comfort Food bezeichnet Küchenchef Michael Ferraro die beliebten Klassiker mit einer Prise Innovation, die bei ihm auf der Karte stehen. Seine Version eines Imbisses ebnete den Weg für eine neue Generation des amerikanischen Delicatessen-Konzeptes, kurz Deli, und verpasste dem etwas angestaubten Image eine Verjüngungs-Kur. Das Architekturbüro nemaworkshop lieferte seinen Beitrag in Form einer loftartigen Location mit Edelstahlfassade, deren „Garagentore" aus Glas komplett geöffnet werden können, um die Grenzen zwischen Innen und Außen aufzuheben. Im Untergeschoss befinden sich eine gepolsterte Lounge mit einem Glasdach zum Hinterhof und einem Wandgemälde von Künstler Juan José Heredia sowie eine Bar für abendliche Drinks.

Ce restaurant, situé entre les quartiers SoHo et NoLIta de Manhattan, est apprécié pour sa cuisine sans fioriture et son atmosphère détendue. Le chef Michael Ferraro propose des aliments-réconfort internationaux, qui sont tous des grands classiques mais auxquels il apporte une touche d'innovation. Son interprétation de la restauration rapide a ouvert la voie à une nouvelle conception du delicatessen américain, aussi connu sous le diminutif de « deli », qui a ainsi retrouvé une seconde jeunesse et est revenu au goût du jour. Le bureau d'architectes nemaworkshop a fait de l'établissement un loft à la façade en acier inoxydable, dont les « portes de garage » en verre peuvent être ouvertes entièrement afin de joindre les espaces intérieur et extérieur. Au sous-sol, vous trouverez un salon aux sièges rembourrés, avec un toit en verre donnant sur la cour arrière, une peinture murale de Juan José Heredia ainsi qu'un bar pour les cocktails du soir.

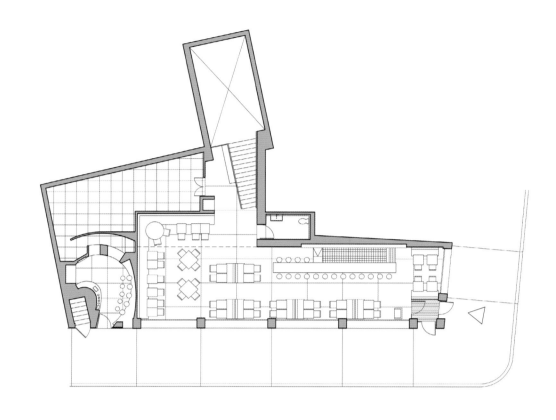

Ember Room

New York, USA

647 Ninth Avenue
New York City, NY 10036

Phone: +1 212 245 8880
www.emberroom.com

Prices: $$
Cuisine: Asian

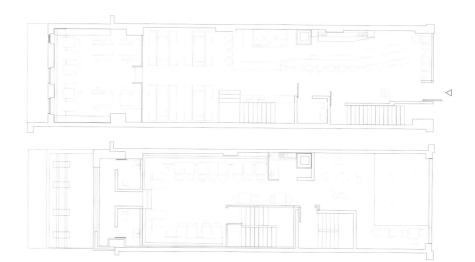

Architecture/Design
Roy Nachum
www.roynachum.com

Photos
Kapil Gandhi/Full Lock Media

4,000 Thai bells with heart-shaped Bodhi tree leaves hang from the ceiling. Asian characters glow on the walls. In contrast, the furniture is clearly minimalistic. As is the case in the design of the two-story restaurant, two culinary worlds meet in the Ember Room. Celebrity chef Todd English and his colleague Pongtawat Chalermkittichai from Thailand join forces in the kitchen and blend American barbeque with Asian herbs and spices. Artist and designer Roy Nachum is responsible for the interior design. Nachum used dark wood extensively, combined with natural materials such as volcanic rock and clay bricks. He paneled some of the walls with unfinished wood. Nachum also painted the elephant picture that dominates the room.

4 000 thailändische Glöckchen mit herzförmigen Bodhibaumblättern hängen von der Decke. An den Wänden leuchten asiatische Schriftzeichen. Das Mobiliar dagegen ist klar und minimalistisch. Genau wie beim Design des zweistöckigen Restaurants treffen im Ember Room auch kulinarisch zwei Welten aufeinander. In der Küche stehen Promikoch Todd English und sein Kollege Pongtawat Chalermkittichai aus Thailand. Sie mixen amerikanisches Barbecue mit asiatischen Kräutern und Gewürzen. Die Einrichtung kommt von Künstler und Designer Roy Nachum. Er verwendete viel dunkles Holz, bediente sich natürlicher Materialien wie Vulkanstein und Lehmziegel. Die Wände verkleidete er teilweise mit unbearbeitetem Holz. Nachum malte auch das raumbeherrschende Elefanten-Bild.

Au plafond pendent 4 000 petites cloches thaïlandaises, toutes décorées de feuilles d'arbre de la Bodhi en forme de cœur. Les murs sont parsemés de signes asiatiques illuminés. En opposition à ce décor stylé, le mobilier est clair et minimaliste. Deux mondes contrastés qui s'affrontent autant dans le design de ce restaurant de deux étages que dans les mets culinaires proposés. Le maître aux fourneaux n'est autre que le grand chef Todd English, secondé de son collègue thaïlandais Pongtawat Chalermkittichai. Ils allient barbecue américain aux épices et fines herbes asiatiques. La décoration porte la griffe de l'artiste et designer Roy Nachum, qui a opté pour du bois foncé et des matériaux naturels tels que la pierre volcanique et la brique en limon. Les murs partiellement recouverts de bois brut constituent le support de l'imposante peinture d'éléphant.

The Wright

New York, USA

at the Guggenheim Museum, 1071 Fifth Avenue
New York City, NY 10128

Phone: +1 212 427 5690
www.thewrightrestaurant.com

Prices: $$
Cuisine: American-International

Architecture/Design
Andre Kikoski Architect
www.akarch.com

Photos
Peter Aaron

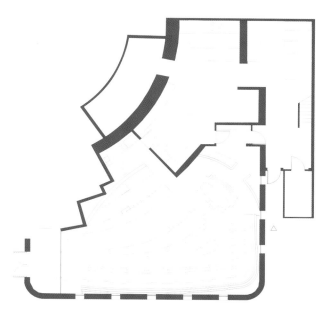

For architect Andre Kikoski, designing the restaurant in Frank Lloyd Wright's Guggenheim Museum was a huge stroke of luck—and the biggest challenge of his career up to that point. He tried to imagine how the star architect, who died in 1959, would have designed the space. Wright would have certainly used the most modern materials available. Wherever possible, Kikoski used energy-efficient LEDs. They provide the backlighting for the wall elements made of walnut, and they also highlight the characteristic ceiling canopy. Along the wall, a sweeping banquette upholstered in blue outlines the contour of the room. A bar clad in metal and topped with Corian has a curve as dynamic as the entire room.

Für Architekt Andre Kikoski war die Einrichtung des Restaurants in Frank Lloyd Wrights Guggenheim Museum der größte Glücksfall und zugleich die größte Heraus-forderung seiner bisherigen Karriere. Er stellte sich vor, wie der 1959 verstorbene Star-Architekt den Raum gestaltet hätte. Auch Wright hätte sich wohl der modernsten zur Verfügung stehenden Materialien bedient. Wo immer es möglich war, setzte Kikoski energiesparende LEDs ein. Sie hinterleuchten zum Beispiel die Wandelemente aus Walnussholz und setzen die charakteristische Deckenverkleidung in Szene. Eine blaubezogene Sitzbank entlang der Wand gibt dem Raum eine klare Kontur. Die Bar ist aus Metall und einer Arbeitsplatte aus Corian gefertigt und ebenso dynamisch gebogen wie der gesamte Raum.

L'occasion pour l'architecte Andre Kikoski d'aménager le restaurant du Musée Guggenheim de Frank Lloyd Wright était à la fois une chance inouïe et un réel défi pour sa carrière. Il s'est imaginé comment l'architecte de renom décédé en 1959 aurait agencé la pièce. Wright aurait sûrement opté pour les matériaux disponibles les plus modernes. Dans la mesure du possible, Kikoski a opté pour des lampes LEDs économes pour notamment illuminer les éléments muraux en noyer et mettre en scène la décoration du plafond assez caractéristique. Le banc mural recouvert d'un tissu bleu délimite l'espace où l'on peut admirer un bar constitué de métal et d'un plan de travail en Corian à la forme tout aussi dynamique que l'ensemble de la pièce.

Beauty & Essex

New York, USA

146 Essex Street
New York City, NY 10002

Phone: +1 212 614 0146
www.beautyandessex.com

Prices: $$$
Cuisine: American-International

Architecture/Design
AvroKO
www.avroko.com

Photos
courtesy of AvroKO

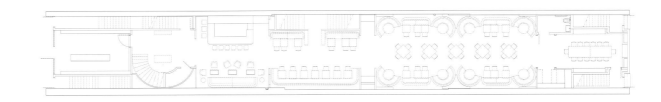

When passing by, this store looks like a higher-end pawnshop on New York's Lower East Side that specializes in electric guitars and odds and ends from the '80s. Beyond the backdoor, however, a completely different world reveals itself to patrons. A chic staircase illuminated by an enormous chandelier leads to a space with an ambience that falls somewhere between an intimate boudoir and a speakeasy from the days of Al Capone. Pocket watches, dim lighting, Chesterfield upholstery, and crystal carafes pay homage to a bygone era when all gentlemen wore hats and women would meet in the powder room for a chat. Back in those days, members of the high society would gather in such establishments to enjoy bootleg liquor; today, the young and hip come to indulge in first-class cocktails and the best of contemporary crossover cuisine.

Im Vorbeilaufen wirkt der Laden wie ein besseres Pfandhaus der New Yorker Lower East Side, spezialisiert auf E-Gitarren und Krimskrams aus den 80ern. Jenseits der Hintertür offenbart sich dem Gast jedoch eine gänzlich andere Welt. Ein mondäner Treppenaufgang, erhellt von einem enormen Lüster, führt in eine Atmosphäre zwischen intimem Boudoir und Speakeasy zu Zeiten von Al Capone. Taschenuhren, schummriges Licht, Chesterfield-Polster und Kristallkaraffen wirken wie eine Hommage an eine vergangene Ära, in der jeder Gentleman Hut trug und sich die Damen auf einen Plausch im „Powder Room" trafen. Zu damaligen Zeiten gesellte sich in solchen Etablissements die High Society zum verbotenen Drink, heute versammelt sich ein junges Szenepublikum zum unbeschwerten Genuss erstklassiger Cocktails und dem Besten aus der modernen Crossover-Küche.

De l'extérieur, le local a plutôt l'air d'une maison de prêt sur gage du Lower East Side new-yorkais spécialisée dans les guitares électriques et les babioles des années 80. Une fois la porte de derrière franchie, en revanche, un monde complètement différent s'ouvre aux convives. Un grand escalier surplombé d'un énorme lustre vous fait pénétrer dans une atmosphère à mi-chemin entre un boudoir intime et un bar clandestin de l'époque d'Al Capone. Montres de poche, faible luminosité, canapés Chesterfield et carafes de cristal semblent rendre hommage à une époque révolue, où chaque homme portait un borsalino et où les femmes bavardaient entre elles tout en se repoudrant. Alors que la haute société raffolait de ces établissements du temps de la prohibition, c'est aujourd'hui un public jeune qui vient profiter de succulents cocktails et de plats internationaux modernes.

Distrito

Philadelphia, USA

3945 Chestnut Street
Philadelphia, PA 19104

Phone: +1 215 222 1657
www.distritorestaurant.com

Prices: $$
Cuisine: Mexican

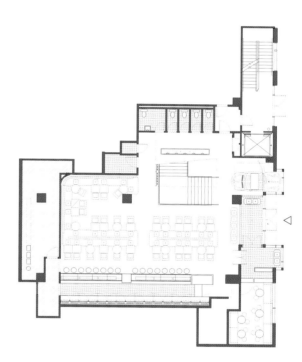

Architecture/Design
Jun Aizaki/crème design
www.cremedesign.com

Photos
Fanny Allié
www.fannyallie.com

All it takes is one look at this two-story restaurant to realize that this is no typical Tex-Mex bar that serves nachos with cheese dip and Corona beer. With a striking design that is a mixture of an American diner, Mexican wrestling, and a candy vending machine, this restaurant has established an entirely new genre in Philadelphia's gastronomy scene. Owner Jose Garces has seen to that. Under his management, the kitchen prepares authentic Latin American dishes such as tortilla soup, ceviche, and huarache, a Mexican version of pizza. Sometime after your second pitcher of margaritas and a round of karaoke, how the wrestling masks, pink cushions, and a VW beetle all hang together will become a bit fuzzy—what you'll remember, however, is an evening in one of the coolest restaurants in the world.

Schon beim ersten Blick in das zweistöckige Restaurant wird deutlich: Dies ist keine typische Tex-Mex-Bar, die Nachos mit Käsedip und Corona-Bier serviert. Der Laden mit seinem plakativen Thema, das wie eine Kreuzung aus amerikanischem Diner, mexikanischem Kampfsport und einem Bonbonautomaten daherkommt, entpuppt sich als ein gänzlich neues Genre in Philadelphias Gastroszene. Dafür sorgt Besitzer Jose Garces, unter dessen Leitung die Köche authentische lateinamerikanische Gerichte wie Tortilla-Suppe, Ceviche und Huarache, eine mexikanische Version der Pizza, zubereiten. Spätestens nach dem zweiten Margarita-Pitcher und einer Runde Karaoke verlieren die genauen Zusammenhänge zwischen Lucha-Libre-Masken, pinken Polstern und einem VW Käfer an Bedeutung – was bleibt, ist die Erinnerung an einen Abend in einem der coolsten Restaurants der Welt.

Il suffit d'un regard pour comprendre que ce restaurant de deux étages n'est pas un bar Tex-Mex typique, servant des nachos avec de la sauce au fromage et de la bière Corona. Sa décoration exubérante mêle les genres dans un concept frappant : diner américain, sports de combat mexicains et distributeurs de bonbons. Sous l'égide de Jose Garces, l'établissement a inventé un genre nouveau dans le paysage gastronomique de Philadelphie. Les cuisiniers préparent d'authentiques plats d'Amérique latine tels que la soupe de tortillas, le céviche et le huarache, version mexicaine de la pizza. Après le deuxième pichet de margarita et la première session de karaoké, le rapport entre les masques de lucha libre, les coussins roses et la voiture coccinelle perd généralement tout son sens. Qu'importe, il reste le souvenir d'une soirée dans l'un des restaurants les plus sympathiques au monde.

Gitane

San Francisco, USA

6 Claude Lane
San Francisco, CA 94108

Phone: +1 415 788 6686
www.gitanerestaurant.com

Prices: $$
Cuisine: Catalan

Architecture/Design
Mister Important Design
www.misterimportant.com

Photos
Jeff Dow

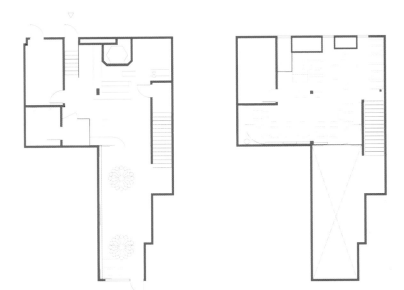

The entrance alone makes hippie hearts beat faster: Large graffiti flowers decorate the brick façade and the restaurant's logo. The floral patterns of the flower children continue in the rooms—on the upholstered seats of the bar stools, for instance. The influences of different cultures can be seen in the furnishings of Gitane, just as they can be found in the culture of gypsies after which the restaurant is named. Interior designers at Mister Important Design combined vintage chandeliers with hand-printed wallpapers, and kitschy tapestries with a solid wooden bar and a cabinet with dusty wine bottles. The result can be described as organized chaos. The menu is an equally wild potpourri: The dishes are a mixture of Spanish, French, and Middle Eastern ingredients.

Schon der Eingang lässt Hippie-Herzen höher schlagen: Große Blumen-Graffitis zieren die Backsteinfassade und das Logo des Restaurants. In den Räumen finden sich ebenfalls die floralen Muster der Blumenkinder wieder, zum Beispiel auf den Bezügen der Barhocker. Genau wie in der Kultur der Zigeuner finden sich auch in der Einrichtung des Gitane die Einflüsse verschiedener Kulturen. Die Innenarchitekten der Agentur Mister Important kombinierten Vintage-Leuchter zu handbedruckten Tapeten, kitschige Wandbehänge zu einer soliden Holztheke und einer Vitrine mit angestaubten Weinflaschen. Das Ergebnis lässt sich als geordnetes Chaos bezeichnen. Ein ebenso wildes Potpourri ist übrigens die Speisekarte. In den Gerichten treffen spanische, französische und orientalische Zutaten aufeinander.

L'entrée de ce restaurant fera déjà battre le cœur des hippies avec sa façade de briques décorée de graffitis de fleurs, que l'on retrouve également dans le graphisme du logo. L'intérieur fait également honneur au style des « enfants fleurs » puisque l'on retrouve les mêmes motifs sur le revêtement des tabourets du bar. À l'image de la culture gitane, la multiculturalité est omniprésente dans l'aménagement du Gitane. Les architectes d'intérieur de l'agence Mister Important ont combiné des lampes vintage avec des tapisseries artisanales, des revêtements muraux kitchs avec un bar en bois massif et une vitrine de vins poussiéreux. Le tout donne naissance à un chaos ordonné. La carte du menu est un pot-pourri sauvage où s'entremêlent des ingrédients espagnols, français et orientaux.

Concrete Blonde

Sydney, Australia

33 Bayswater Road
Sydney, NSW 2011

Phone: +61 2 9380 8307
www.concreteblonderestaurant.com.au

Prices: $$$
Cuisine: Fusion

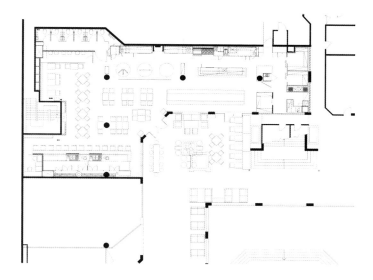

Architecture/Design
Dreamtime Australia Design
www.dreamtimeaustraliadesign.com

Photos
Paul Gosney for Elbow-Room

Michael McCann from Dreamtime Australia Design extensively used rich metal finishes and warm timber for the interior: Firewood stored in polished stainless cylinders adds texture and excitement, while the open circular grills and rotisserie are the true heart of this restaurant. Here, chef Ian Oakes serves innovative dishes using local ingredients. A glassed-in, air-conditioned wine cellar stores an exquisite selection of international wines. The ceiling has exposed structural concrete beams with recycled acoustical flocking, and custom spun aluminum spheres decorate the 30-foot bar. On the terrace, guests sit on eclectic illuminated furniture under the contemporary graffiti awning where they can admire a custom fire and water feature. On their way to the restrooms, a pop-art-style mosaic beauty greets guests.

Michael McCann vom Designbüro Dreamtime Australia hat sich für die Einrichtung vor allem auf Metalloberflächen und warmes Holz konzentriert: Das Feuerholz lagert in polierten Metallzylindern und verleiht dem Raum eine reizvolle Struktur, während die offenen Grillstationen der Mittelpunkt des Restaurants sind. Chef-koch Ian Oakes serviert hier innovative Gerichte mit lokalen Zutaten. Die exquisite, internationale Weinauswahl steht in geometrisch angeordneten Regalen in einem mit Glas abgetrennten Kühler. An den Decken verlaufen mit Faserzement verkleidete Belüftungsrohre, und symmetrisch angeordnete Metallkugeln bilden die Frontseite der neun Meter langen Bar. Auf der Terrasse sitzt man unter einer Graffiti-Markise auf illuminierten Kunststoffmöbeln, daneben spuckt eine Fontaine wahlweise Feuer oder Wasser. Der Weg zur Toilette ist ein Highlight: Eine Mosaik-Schönheit im Pop-Art-Stil grüßt die Gäste.

Le designer Michael McCann de l'agence Dreamtime Australia a opté pour une décoration principalement composée de métal et de bois : le bois du feu est entreposé dans des cylindres métalliques et confère à l'endroit une structure fascinante, alors que les grills ouverts constituent le point central du restaurant. Le chef Ian Oakes propose des plats novateurs avec des ingrédients locaux. L'exquise sélection de vins internationaux est présentée sur des étagères géométriques dans une armoire en verre réfrigérante. Au plafond, on peut admirer les conduits d'aération revêtus de fibrociment et les boules en métal symétriques qui constituent la façade du bar de neuf mètres de long. La terrasse avec sa marquise décorée de graffitis et ses meubles en PVC illuminés attend les invités qui pourront admirer la fontaine centrale où le feu et l'eau s'alternent. L'allée menant aux toilettes vaut le détour : les invités sont accueillis par une belle mosaïque de style pop art.

Tote on the Turf

Mumbai, India

Mahalaxmi Race Course, opposite Gate 5 & 6, Keshva Rao Khadye Marg
Mumbai, 400034

Phone: +91 22 6157 7777
www.thetote.in

Prices: $$$
Cuisine: Modern Indian

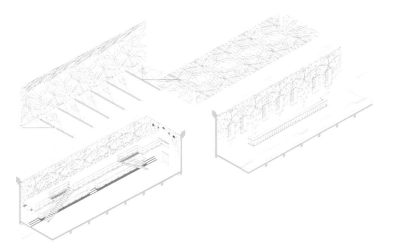

Architecture/Design
Serie Architects
www.serie.co.uk

Photos
Fram Petit

Rahul Akerkar, whose hospitality company deGustibus already owns Mumbai's well-known restaurant Indigo, is also the creative mind behind Tote on the Turf, a restaurant that guarantees sophisticated cuisine. This sprawling project at Mahalaxmi Racecourse encompasses almost 25,000 square feet and includes a grill restaurant, an outdoor area, banquet rooms, and a bar whose architecture was recognized with the Wallpaper Design Award. Christopher Lee's and Kapil Gupta's designs were inspired by the branching crowns of the surrounding rain trees, and their shapes are repeated in the building structures and the bar's laser-cut wall paneling. Signature cocktails such as the Tote Mary help to while away the time waiting for one of the coveted tables in the restaurant. During the racing season, members of the city's high society meet at Tote on the Turf, and reservations are recommended.

Rahul Akerkar, zu dessen Gastrounternehmen deGustibus bereits Mumbais bekanntes Restaurant Indigo gehört, ist auch der kreative Kopf hinter Tote on the Turf, was eine anspruchsvolle Küche garantiert. Das Projekt an der Mahalaxmi Pferderennbahn erstreckt sich über rund 2 300 Quadratmeter Fläche und beinhaltet ein Grillrestaurant, einen Außenbereich, Banketträume und eine Bar, deren Architektur mit dem Wallpaper Design Award ausgezeichnet wurde. Christopher Lee und Kapil Gupta wurden von den verzweigten Kronen der umliegenden Regenbäume zu ihren Entwürfen inspiriert, deren Formensprache sich in den Gebäudeträgern und der lasergeschnittenen Wandverkleidung der Bar wiederfindet. Hauseigene Cocktails wie die „Tote Mary" verkürzen die Wartezeit auf einen der begehrten Tische im Restaurant. Während der Rennsaison trifft sich im Tote on the Turf die High Society der Stadt, und eine Reservierung ist empfehlenswert.

Rahul Akerkar est le propriétaire de la société de restauration deGustibus dont le restaurant Indigo, à Mumbai, est une enseigne célèbre. C'est également lui qui se cache derrière le Tote on the Turf, ce qui garantit l'excellence de la cuisine. L'établissement s'étend sur près de 2 300 mètres carrés au bord de l'hippodrome de Mahalaxmi et comprend un restaurant grill, un espace extérieur, des salles de banquet et un bar dont l'architecture a été primée du Wallpaper Design Award. Christopher Lee et Kapil Gupta se sont inspirés des cimes abondantes des arbres à pluie environnants, dont la forme se retrouve dans les poutres du bâtiment et le revêtement, travaillé au laser, des murs du bar. Des cocktails maisons tels que le « Tote Mary » font passer l'attente avant de pouvoir passer à l'une des tables très prisées du restaurant. La haute société de Mumbai se retrouvant volontiers au Tote on the Turf durant la saison hippique, il est recommandé de réserver.

Blue Frog

Mumbai, India

Mathuradas Mills Compound, Senapati Bapat Marg
Mumbai, 400013

Phone: +91 22 6158 6158
www.bluefrog.co.in

Prices: $$$
Cuisine: International

Architecture/Design
Serie Architects
www.serie.co.uk

Photos
Fram Petit

Planned as a bar, lounge, restaurant, club, and concert room alike, the Blue Frog was a challenge for the team from Serie Architects. The designers refer to the location's concept as "acoustic lounge," and its walls are indeed reminiscent of an oversized sound studio. The terraced design of the seating area is multifunctional. Booths paneled in mahogany seat up to ten people and are staggered on different levels, providing unimpeded views of the stage. Backlit acrylic glass fills the spaces between the booths, creating privacy for guests as well as providing the primary lighting for the room. Through a glass panel, diners can watch as chefs prepare grilled dishes, curries, and international cuisine. The highlight of the Blue Frog is its musical entertainment with well-known live acts and DJs from around the world.

Gleichermaßen als Bar, Lounge, Restaurant, Club und Konzertraum geplant, war das Blue Frog eine Herausforderung für das Team von Serie Architects. „Acoustic Lounge" nennen die Designer das Konzept der Location, deren Wände an ein überdimensionales Tonstudio erinnern. Multifunktionalität zeigt sich auch in der terrassenartigen Konstruktion des Sitzbereichs. Bis zu zehn Personen finden in den mit Mahagoniholz ausgekleideten Boxen Platz, deren ansteigende Anordnung für ungehinderte Bühnensicht sorgt. Zwischenräume aus Acrylglas bewahren die Privatsphäre der Gäste und formen das zentrale Leuchtobjekt des Raumes. Durch eine Glasfront kann man den Köchen bei der Zubereitung von Gegrilltem, Currys und internationalen Gerichten zusehen. Das Highlight des Blue Frog ist sein musikalisches Unterhaltungsprogramm mit bekannten Live-Acts und DJs aus aller Welt.

Prévu pour être à la fois bar, lounge, restaurant, boîte de nuit et salle de concert, le Blue Frog a représenté un défi de taille pour les designers de Serie Architects, qui ont nommé leur concept « Acoustic Lounge ». Le lieu ressemble à un studio d'enregistrement géant, et sa multifonctionnalité est soulignée par l'aménagement des sièges. Dix personnes peuvent prendre place aux tables en acajou placées dans des sortes d'alvéoles, dont l'agencement en dénivelé permet une vue parfaite de la scène. Le plexiglas délimitant ces alvéoles garantit l'intimité des convives tout en fournissant la principale source de lumière de la salle. Une vitre permet d'observer les cuisiniers dans la préparation de grillades, currys et plats internationaux. Le principal atout du Blue Frog est cependant son programme musical de par sa capacité à attirer des stars ou des DJs renommés.

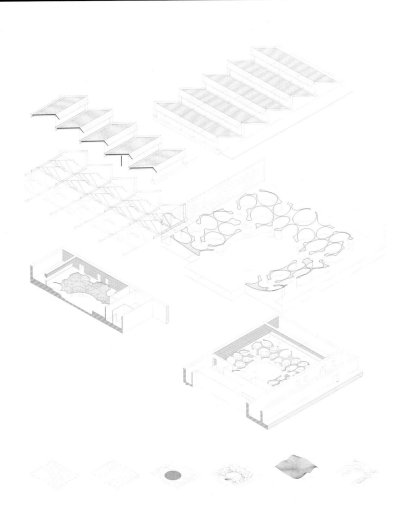

Smoke House Deli

New Delhi, India

Shop 125, DLF Promenade Mall, Nelson Mandela Marg, Vasant Kunj
New Delhi, 110070

Phone: +91 11 4607 5646

Prices: $$
Cuisine: International

Architecture/Design
THEBUSRIDE Design Studio
www.jointhebusride.com

Photos
courtesy of IEHPL

It is said that The Busride Design Studio team spent night and day drawing the pictures on the walls of the Smoke House Deli and didn't finish until shortly before the opening. Among other things, the drawings depict a life-sized wall clock, television, and fireplace and give the restaurant's design a touch of irony. The interior can be described as a blend of colonial style and modern design. Diners sit at dark wood tables in '50s-style shell chairs. Ventilation ducts painted white run along the ceiling alongside black chandeliers featuring lampshades with stylized chandelier punch-outs. Garden fences separate the tables, providing diners with privacy. The menu features European and international dishes.

Nächtelang und noch bis kurz vor der Eröffnung soll das Team von The Busride Design Studio die Bilder an den Wänden des Smoke House Deli gezeichnet haben. Sie zeigen eine Wanduhr, einen Fernseher oder einen Kamin in Originalgröße und ergänzen auf diese Weise mit einer Prise Ironie die Einrichtung des Restaurants. Sie lässt sich als eine Mischung aus Kolonialstil und modernem Design beschreiben. Man sitzt in Schalensesseln im Stil der 50er Jahre an dunklen Holztischen. An der Decke verlaufen weiß gestrichene Belüftungsrohre. Daneben hängen schwarze Leuchten, aus deren Lampenschirmen stilisierte Kronleuchter ausgestanzt sind. Gartenzäune trennen die Tische voneinander und geben den Gästen Privatsphäre. Auf der Karte stehen europäische und internationale Gerichte.

L'équipe du The Busride Design Studio a passé des nuits entières, jusqu'à la veille de l'ouverture, à peindre les images grandeur nature sur les murs du Smoke House Deli. Elles représentent une horloge murale, un téléviseur ou une cheminée et complètent l'aménagement intérieur du restaurant avec une touche d'ironie, ce dernier mêlant style colonial et design moderne. Assis dans des fauteuils ronds des années 50 à des tables en bois foncé, vous pourrez contempler la blancheur des conduits d'aération du plafond et les lampes noires dont les abat-jours stylés portent une gravure de lustre. Des clôtures de jardin séparent chaque table et confèrent aux clients un peu d'intimité. La carte propose des plats européens et internationaux.

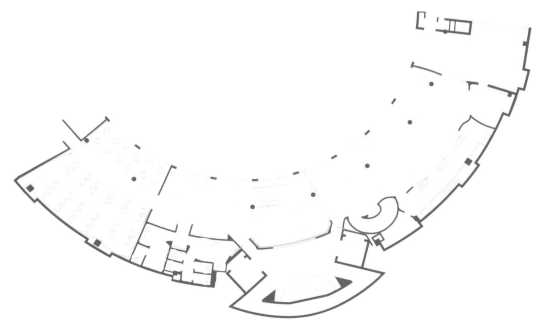

SEVVA

Hong Kong, China

Prince's Building 25/F, 10 Chater Road
Hong Kong

Phone: +852 2537 1388
www.sevva.hk

Prices: $$$
Cuisine: International

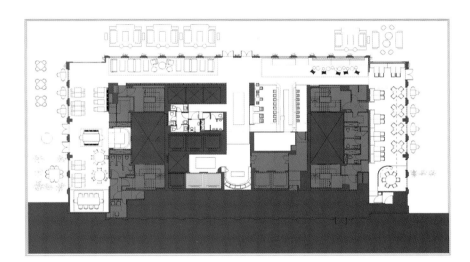

Architecture/Design
Tsao & McKown Architects
www.tsao-mckown.com

Photos
Virgile Simon Bertrand

Apparently even dyed-in-the-wool Hong Kong natives never get tired of looking at the panorama of their city. Founded by style icon Bonnie Gokson and located on the 25th floor of a major retail and office building, Sevva has a 360-degree view of the city's skyline. Gokson, entrepreneur and former head of image and communications for Chanel Asia Pacific, hired the New York office of Tsao & McKown Architects to handle the expansion. Calvin Tsao, a native of this Chinese metropolis, divided the rooms into a half dozen different areas. A gigantic chandelier hanging over a display case appears to mirror the shape of the cakes presented underneath. Sofas, armchairs, and sitting areas are upholstered in bright, coordinating fabrics. The strict character of the elegantly set tables, all in white, is further enhanced by the images of German photographer Candida Höfer.

Angeblich können sich selbst eingefleischte Bewohner Hongkongs nicht satt sehen an dem Panorama ihrer Stadt. Das Restaurant Sevva von Stilikone Bonnie Gokson bietet mit seinem 360-Grad-Ausblick beste Bedingungen. Es befindet sich im 25. Stock eines wichtigen Einkaufs- und Bürogebäudes. Mit dem Ausbau beauftragte die Unternehmerin und ehemalige PR-Chefin von Chanel Asia das New Yorker Büro Tsao & McKown Architects. Calvin Tsao, der selbst aus der chinesischen Metropole stammt, hat die Räume in ein halbes Dutzend verschiedener Bereiche aufgeteilt. Ein gigantischer Leuchter über der Bar scheint mit der Form der darunter präsentierten Torten zu korrespondieren. Sofas, Sessel und Sitzecken sind jeweils mit aufeinander abgestimmten, bunten Stoffen bezogen. Der strikte Charakter der in Weiß gedeckten Tische wird durch die Bilder der deutschen Fotografin Candida Höfer noch verstärkt.

Même les plus anciens habitants de Hong Kong ne peuvent, paraît-il, se lasser de contempler le paysage offert par leur ville. Le restaurant Sevva a tout du lieu idéal pour cela grâce à sa vue panoramique à 360°. Propriété de Bonnie Gokson, icône de style, il est situé au 25ème étage d'un bâtiment commercial et administratif. L'entrepreneuse et ancienne responsable d'image et communication de Chanel Asia a chargé le bureau new-yorkais Tsao & McKown Architects de l'aménagement. Calvin Tsao, lui aussi originaire de la métropole chinoise, a partagé les salles en une demi-douzaine d'espaces différents. Au-dessus du bar, une gigantesque lampe épouse la même forme que les gâteaux qu'elle surplombe. Les canapés, fauteuils et sièges sont recouverts de tissus multicolores assortis, tandis que l'aspect strict des tables blanches est renforcé par les photographies de l'Allemande Candida Höfer.

208 Duecento Otto

Hong Kong, China

208 Hollywood Road
Hong Kong

Phone: +852 2549 0208
www.208.com.hk

Prices: $$
Cuisine: Italian

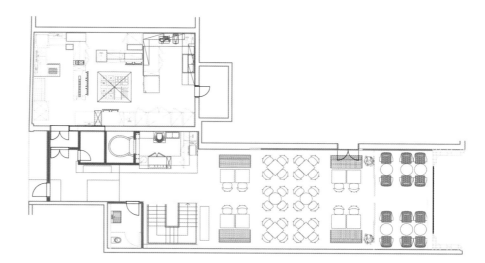

Architecture/Design
Autoban
www.autoban212.com

Photos
George Mitchell

It is no longer unusual for an architectural firm from Istanbul to design an Italian restaurant in Hong Kong. The recipient of numerous awards, 208 Duecento Otto demonstrates how influences from different cultures can work together to enrich a joint project. The wood-fired pizza oven recessed in a wall covered with chinoiserie tiles is a beautiful example of the fusion of Western and Eastern aesthetics. After walking through the bar area with leather bar stools and a relaxed atmosphere, you pass the private dining room before reaching the upper area that exhibits a more rustic charm. Both floors of the former meat storage warehouse have a covered outdoor area surrounded by an illuminated iron façade with a rusty patina. The award-winning stone-oven pizza from Duecento Otto is considered to be the best in the city.

Es ist inzwischen nicht mehr ungewöhnlich, wenn ein Architekturbüro aus Istanbul ein italienisches Restaurant in Hongkong plant. Das mehrfach ausgezeichnete 208, oder Duecento Otto, beweist, wie bereichernd sich die Einflüsse verschiedener Kulturen auf ein gemeinsames Projekt auswirken können. Ein schönes Bild für die Verschmelzung westlicher und östlicher Ästhetik ist der mit Holz befeuerte Pizzaofen, eingelassen in eine Wand aus Chinoiserie-Kacheln. Durch den Bar-Bereich mit Lederhockern und legerer Atmosphäre, vorbei am Private Dining Room, gelangt man in den oberen Bereich von eher rustikalem Charme. Beide Etagen des ehemaligen Fleischlagerhauses verfügen über einen überdachten Außenbereich, umrandet von einer illuminierten Eisenfassade mit rostiger Patina. Die preisgekrönte Steinofenpizza des Duecento Otto gilt als die beste der Stadt.

Il n'y a plus rien d'étonnant à voir un bureau d'architectes d'Istanbul diriger un projet de restaurant italien à Hong Kong. Le 208 – ou Duecento Otto –, plusieurs fois récompensé, prouve à quel point le mélange des cultures peut être enrichissant. Le four à pizza, chauffé au bois et encastré dans un mur carrelé de chinoiseries, symbolise à merveille la fusion entre l'esthétisme occidental et oriental. Derrière le bar avec ses tabourets en cuir et son atmosphère légère, au-delà de la salle à manger privée, le charme rustique de la partie supérieure du restaurant s'ouvre aux convives. Les deux étages de cet ancien dépôt de viande disposent en outre d'un espace extérieur couvert, délimité par une façade de fer illuminée, à la patine rouillée. Les pizzas cuites au four à pierre ont remporté plusieurs prix et sont considérées comme les meilleures de la ville.

Ozone

Hong Kong, China

at Ritz-Carlton Hotel, 1 Austin Road West
Hong Kong

Phone: +852 2263 2263
www.ritzcarlton.com/hongkong

Prices: $$
Cuisine: Asian

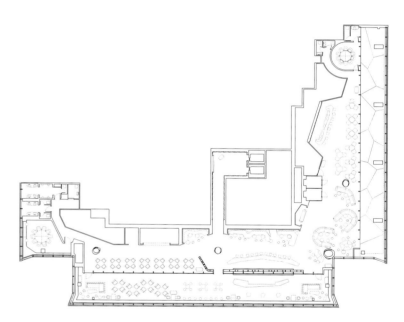

Architecture/Design
Wonderwall Inc.
www.wonder-wall.com

Photos
Nacása & Partners Inc.

No other hotel comes closer to the protective atmosphere surrounding our planet than the Ritz-Carlton in Hong Kong. Considering its name, it's fitting that the bar complete with lounge and restaurant is located at the top (the 118th floor) of the International Commerce Centre in Kowloon. Against this backdrop, Wonderwall set itself the goal of coming up with a truly epic design for the interior of this space. References to human nature and its development can be found in the recurrent cell patterns on the floor, ceiling, shelving units, and even the walls of the elevator. Marble used extensively throughout the space organically reflects these cell structures and fits into the overall concept despite its massive presence. Changing lighting moods visually separate the bar, lounge, dining room, sushi bar, two private VIP rooms, as well as an outdoor area.

Kein anderes Hotel kommt näher an die schützende Gasschicht, die den Erdball umgibt, als das Ritz-Carlton in Hongkong. Treffend erscheint da der Name der Bar mit Lounge und Restaurant im obersten, dem 118. Stockwerk des International Commerce Centre in Kowloon. Unter diesen Voraussetzungen hat sich Wonderwall zum Ziel gesetzt, eine Innenarchitektur von epischem Ausmaß zu entwerfen. Referenzen zur menschlichen Natur und deren Entstehung finden sich in einem immer wiederkehrenden Zellenmuster in Boden, Decke, Regalelementen und den Wänden des Aufzugs. Auf natürliche Weise greift der häufig verwendete Marmor diese Strukturen auf und fügt sich trotz massiver Formen in das Gesamtbild ein. Wechselnde Lichtstimmungen schaffen eine optische Unterteilung von Bar, Lounge, Speiseraum, Sushibar und zwei privaten VIP-Räumen sowie einem Außenbereich.

Le Ritz-Carlton de Hong Kong est l'hôtel le plus haut du monde et ainsi le plus proche de la couche de gaz qui entoure et protège notre planète. Dès lors, le nom du bar avec lounge et restaurant situé au 118ème et dernier étage de l'International Commerce Centre, à Kowloon, paraît des plus appropriés. Wonderwall s'est fixé pour objectif de fournir une dimension grandiose à l'intérieur, en adéquation avec la symbolique du lieu. Les références à la nature humaine et ses origines se retrouvent à l'infini dans le sol, le plafond, les étagères et les murs de l'ascenseur. Le marbre, souvent utilisé, embellit ces structures et s'intègre parfaitement malgré ses formes massives. Différentes ambiances lumineuses créent une division optique du bar, du lounge, de la salle de repas, du bar à sushis, des deux salles VIP ainsi que de l'espace extérieur.

Fairwood Buddies Café

Hong Kong, China

Shop 18, Podium First Floor, Caribbean Bazaar, Caribbean Coast
Hong Kong

Phone: +852 2856 4459
www.fairwood.com.hk

Prices: $
Cuisine: Fast-Food

Architecture/Design
Beige Design Ltd.

Photos
Ulso Tsang
courtesy of Beige Design Ltd.

Pythagoras would have truly enjoyed this fast-food restaurant. An unavoidable hexagonal column formed the inspiration for interior designer Danny Chan's entire design concept. By covering the column in mirrors, Chan not only caused the massive column to disappear visually, he also used the reflections themselves as a design element. The walnut veneer wall panels contrast with the restaurant's expanses of cool white and high-tech materials such as the Corian used for the bar. Whether three-dimensional wall coverings, tables, chairs, lamps, or the floor—every detail reflects the concept's hexagonal geometry and was designed and manufactured specifically for this Fairwood restaurant branch. A chain of fast-food restaurants familiar throughout China, Fairwood is popular because of its Asian and Western dishes at affordable prices.

Pythagoras hätte seine wahre Freude an diesem Fast-Food-Restaurant. Ein unumgehbarer Tragpfeiler mit sechseckiger Grundfläche inspirierte Interior Designer Danny Chan dazu, das gesamte Einrichtungskonzept um diesen herum zu gestalten. Mithilfe einer Verkleidung aus Spiegelflächen ließ er die massive Säule optisch verschwinden, um gleichzeitig die Reflektionen als Gestaltungselement zu nutzen. Das Nussbaumfurnier der Wandpaneele kontrastiert zum kühlen Weiß und technischen Materialien wie dem Corian der Bar. Ob dreidimensionale Wandverkleidungen, Tische, Stühle, Lampen oder der Boden – jedes Detail folgt einer hexagonalen Geometrie und wurde eigens für diese Fairwood Filiale entworfen und hergestellt. Die in ganz China verbreitete Kette von Schnellrestaurants ist beliebt wegen ihrer asiatischen und westlichen Gerichte zu bezahlbaren Preisen.

Pythagore aurait rêvé d'un fast-food comme celui-ci. Un imposant pilier hexagonal a poussé le designer d'intérieur Danny Chan à tout aménager selon ce thème. En recouvrant le pilier de miroirs, il a contribué à le faire en quelque sorte disparaître du décor, et il a pu se servir de la réflexion comme d'un élément important dans l'aménagement des lieux. Le bois de noyer des panneaux muraux contraste avec la blancheur froide de certains matériaux, comme le Corian du bar. Les couvertures murales tridimensionnelles, les tables, les chaises, les lampes et le sol ont tous une forme géométrique hexagonale. Tout a été créé et fabriqué sur mesure pour cette filiale de Fairwood. La chaîne de restauration rapide, présente partout en Chine, est particulièrement appréciée pour ses plats asiatiques et occidentaux à des prix abordables.

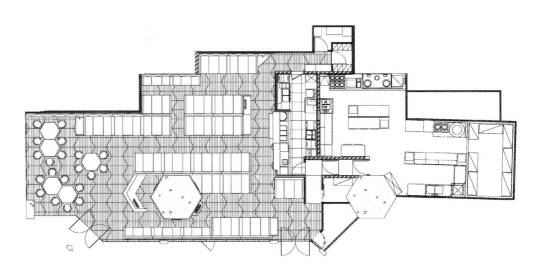

Hōtō Fudō

Yamanashi, Japan

2458 Funatsu, Fujikawaguchiko-machi, Minamitsuru-gun
Yamanashi, 401-0301

Phone: +81 555 72 8511
www.houtou-fudou.jp

Prices: $$
Cuisine: Japanese

Architecture/Design
TAKESHI HOSAKA Architects
www.hosakatakeshi.com

Photos
Koji Fujii/Nacása & Partners Inc.

This restaurant is positioned at the foot of Mount Fuji like a white cave. With its igloo-like shape reminiscent of clouds, it forms a visual contrast to the highest mountain in Japan. When it snows, it fits in symbiotically with the landscape. The interior space is usually open to the elements on all sides, giving guests the feeling that they are sitting outside. Only when the weather is cold and after closing hours are the acrylic sliding doors actually shut. There is no air conditioning, because the structure's steel-concrete shell regulates the temperature. The interior is spartan: Wooden tables, chairs, and benches provide a place for diners to eat regional noodle dishes. Hōtō, by the way, is the name of a traditional noodle soup. Takeshi Hosaka Architects received a number of awards for the building's design, which was completed in 2009.

Wie eine weiße Höhle liegt das Restaurant am Fuße des Mount Fuji. Mit seiner an Wolken erinnernden, igluartigen Form bildet es optisch einen Gegensatz zu dem höchsten Berg Japans. Bei Schnee fügt es sich symbiotisch in die Landschaft ein. Der Innenraum ist die meiste Zeit zu allen Seiten hin offen, sodass die Gäste das Gefühl haben, im Freien zu sitzen. Nur bei kaltem Wetter und nach Ladenschluss werden die Schiebetüren aus Acrylglas geschlossen. Es gibt keine Klimaanlage, denn die Stahlbetonschale des Gebäudes wirkt temperaturregulierend. Die Einrichtung ist spartanisch: Regionale Nudelgerichte – Hōtō ist übrigens der Name einer traditionellen Nudelsuppe – isst man an Tischen mit Stühlen und Bänken aus Holz. Für den Entwurf des 2009 fertiggestellten Gebäudes bekamen Takeshi Hosaka Architects mehrere Auszeichnungen verliehen.

Le restaurant se dresse telle une grotte blanche au pied du mont Fuji. Sa forme à mi-chemin entre nuage et igloo prend le contrepied du plus haut sommet du Japon, et la symbiose avec le paysage est parfaite lorsqu'il neige. L'espace intérieur n'est que très rarement clos, de sorte que les convives ont l'impression d'être assis à l'air libre. Les portes coulissantes en plexiglas ne sont effet fermées que lorsqu'il fait trop froid ou après la fermeture. Le bâtiment n'est pas climatisé car la coque en béton armé permet de réguler la température. La décoration est quant à elle plutôt spartiate : les plats de pâtes régionaux – Hōtō étant le nom d'une soupe traditionnelle – sont servis à des tables, chaises et bancs entièrement en bois. Takeshi Hosaka Architects a reçu plusieurs récompenses pour la conception de ce bâtiment terminé en 2009.

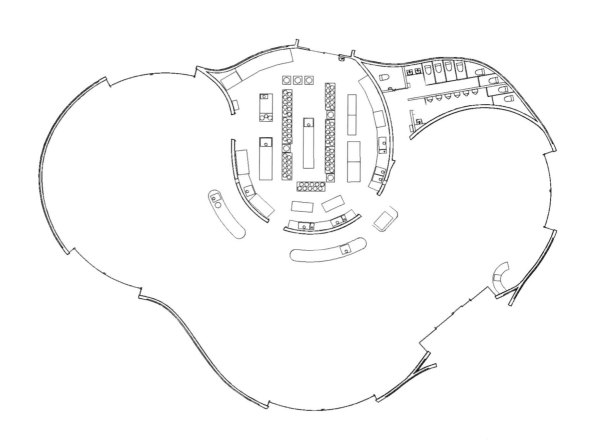

140 Hōtō Fudō

Alice of Magic World

Tokyo, Japan

B3F HALC, Shinjuku West Exit, 1-5-1
Tokyo, 160-0023

Phone: +81 3 3340 2466
www.diamond-dining.com

Prices: $$
Cuisine: International

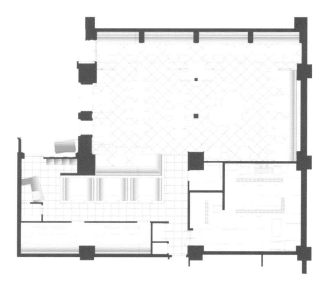

Architecture/Design
Fantastic Design Works
www.f-fantastic.com

Photos
courtesy of Diamond Dining

This restaurant will capture the imaginations of young and old alike. Tokyo-based Fantastic Design Works studio has brought to life the fantasy world from Lewis Carroll's classic novel. At the entrance, oversized books give visitors the feeling of having shrunk. Those who look closer will recognize many episodes from Alice's adventures. In one corner, you feel as if you've been invited to eat with the Queen of Hearts, while in another you dine in the green labyrinth surrounding her castle. Tabletops that look like playing cards, lamps made of hundreds of hearts, and red velvet curtains all look as if they have come from Wonderland. The pizza slices are called Cheshire Cat's tail, and a small chocolate hat crowns the ice cream sundae. By the end of their meal, many diners might imagine that they've caught a glimpse of a white rabbit hurrying by behind a neighboring table.

Dieses Restaurant lässt nicht nur Kinderherzen höherschlagen. Das Studio Fantastic Design Works aus Tokio hat die Phantasiewelt aus Lewis Carrolls Roman zum Leben erweckt. Überdimensionale Bücher am Eingang geben dem Besucher das Gefühl geschrumpft zu sein. Wer genau hinschaut, erkennt viele Episoden der Geschichte von Alice wieder. In einer Ecke fühlt man sich, als sei man von der Herzkönigin zu Tisch geladen, in einer anderen diniert man im grünen Labyrinth ihres Schlosses. Tischplatten in Form von Spielkarten, Lampen aus Hunderten von Herzen oder rote Samtvorhänge scheinen alle dem Wunderland entsprungen zu sein. Sogar die Pizza auf dem Teller ist der Grinsekatze nachempfunden, und den Eisbecher krönt ein kleiner Schokoladenhut. So mancher Gast glaubt am Ende seines Besuchs, er habe hinter dem Nachbartisch ein weißes Kaninchen vorbeihuschen sehen.

Ce restaurant fait battre le cœur des petits et des grands. Et pour cause, puisque le studio Fantastic Design Works de Tokyo a ressuscité le monde fantastique du roman de Lewis Carroll. Dans l'entrée, des livres géants donnent aux visiteurs l'impression d'avoir rapetissé. Les connaisseurs reconnaîtront plusieurs épisodes des histoires d'Alice. Un recoin donne l'impression d'avoir été invité à la table de la Reine de Cœur, un autre de dîner dans le labyrinthe vert de son palais. Les tables en forme de cartes à jouer, les lampes faites de centaines de cœurs, les rideaux de velours rouge : tout semble sortir tout droit du pays des merveilles. Même les pizzas sont inspirées par le chat de Cheshire, et un petit chapeau en chocolat couronne les coupes de glace. À la fin de sa visite, plus d'un convive a l'impression de voir un lapin blanc s'enfuir sous la table voisine.

+green

Tokyo, Japan

1-2-31 Komazawa, Setagaya-ku
Tokyo, 154-0012

Phone: +81 3 3411 6877
www.and-green.jp

Prices: $$
Cuisine: Japanese

Architecture/Design
Sinato Inc.
www.sinato.jp

Photos
Toshiyuki Yano

Chikara Ohno from the architectural firm Sinato specializes in unusual room-in-room solutions. In +green, a restaurant featuring organic vegetarian food, he created several levels on the bottom floor of a three-story apartment house. A small grocery store was constructed on a mezzanine raised 1.5 feet off the ground. Below the mezzanine and extending halfway into the basement is the kitchen. A spiral staircase in a wooden cylinder leads up to the higher level. Its spherical shape is echoed in a white room divider with window-like cutouts. Partition walls of concrete and brick create room-like niches with sleek wooden tables. All these features combine to create an atmosphere almost as intimate as in a private home. When making reservations, you can specify whether you would prefer to sit, for example, in the Cozy Room or in the Green Room.

Chikara Ohno vom Architekturbüro Sinato ist Spezialist für ungewöhnliche Raum-im-Raum-Lösungen. Im vegetarischen Bio-Restaurant +green hat er mehrere Ebenen in die untere Etage eines dreistöckigen Wohnhauses eingezogen. Ein kleiner Lebensmittelladen wurde auf einem Zwischengeschoss etwa einen halben Meter über dem Boden eingerichtet. Darunter befindet sich – zur Hälfte im Souterrain – die Küche. Eine Wendeltreppe führt in einem Holzzylinder auf das obere Level. Die runde Form wird von einem weißen Raumteiler mit fensterähnlichen Aussparungen aufgenommen. Zwischenwände aus Beton und Backstein schaffen zimmerartige Nischen mit schlichten Holztischen. Auf diese Weise ist die Atmosphäre fast so intim wie in einem Privathaus. Bei der Reservierung kann man angeben, ob man beispielsweise lieber im „Cozy Room" oder im „Green Room" sitzen möchte.

Chikara Ohno, du bureau d'architectes Sinato, est spécialiste du concept « pièce dans la pièce ». Il a ainsi aménagé le restaurant bio et végétarien +green sur plusieurs niveaux, au rez-de-chaussée d'une maison de trois étages. Un petit magasin d'alimentation a notamment été installé sur une mezzanine à 50 centimètres au-dessus du sol. La cuisine est située en-dessous, pour moitié au sous-sol. La partie supérieure est accessible par un escalier en bois en colimaçon. Sa forme circulaire se retrouve dans une cloison blanche équipée de petites niches en forme de fenêtres. Des murs en béton et en brique permettent de séparer plusieurs petites pièces meublées de simples tables en bois. L'atmosphère ainsi créée est presque aussi intime que dans une maison normale. Lors de la réservation, le choix vous est laissé entre les différentes pièces, comme la « Cozy Room » ou la « Green Room ».

Jing

Singapore, Singapore

One Fullerton, 1 Fullerton Road
Singapore, 049213

Phone: +65 622 400 88
www.jing.sg

Prices: $$$
Cuisine: Chinese

Architecture/Design
Antonio Eraso Co.
www.antonioeraso.com

Photos
Derek Swalwell

Upon entering Jing, it's the ceiling that catches your eye first: The architects of Antonio Eraso Company have created an unusual ceiling design using golden geometric shapes. The ceiling plays off the sophisticated interior with furniture, floor coverings, and wall finishes in shades of brown and taupe. Jing is particularly proud of its extensive wine cellar: 800 premium wines complement chef Yong Bing Ngen's menu. Fish and seafood are among his specialties. The bottles of wine are stored in a custom-made copper wine cooler that extends from the lobby to the restaurant area. The main room is decorated with an art installation made of acrylic, fabric, and wood by emerging artist Terence Lin, a graduate of the Nanyang Academy of Fine Arts. Two dining niches offer guests privacy.

Der erste Blick im Jing gilt der Decke: Die Architekten der Antonio Eraso Company haben dort eine ungewöhnliche Konstruktion aus goldenen geometrischen Formen angebracht. Sie ergänzt die edle Einrichtung mit Möbeln, Bodenbelag und Wandverkleidung in Braun und Taupe. Besonders stolz ist man im Jing auf die große Weinauswahl: Gut 800 edle Tropfen korrespondieren mit den Gerichten von Chefkoch Yong Bing Ngen. Fisch und Meeresfrüchte gehören zu seinen Spezialitäten. Die Weinflaschen befinden sich in einem maßgefertigten, kupfernen Weinkühler, der von der Rezeption bis in den Restaurantbereich reicht. Eine Installation aus Acryl, Stoff und Holz des Nachwuchskünstlers Terence Lin, Absolvent der Nanyang Academy of Fine Arts, ziert den Hauptraum. Privatsphäre haben die Gäste in den beiden Separees.

Au Jing, le plafond est le premier à attirer l'œil : les architectes d'Antonio Eraso Company y ont imaginé une construction inhabituelle faite de formes géométriques dorées. Elle complète la somptueuse décoration aux couleurs marron et taupe qui se retrouvent dans les meubles, le sol et les murs. Le Jing tire sa fierté de sa sélection de vins : près de 800 breuvages différents accompagnent les plats du chef Yong Bing Ngen, dont les spécialités sont les poissons et les fruits de mer. Les bouteilles se trouvent dans une armoire réfrigérante à vin en cuivre réalisée sur mesure et qui s'étend de la réception à la salle à manger. La décoration de la pièce principale, à base d'acrylique, de tissu et de bois, est l'œuvre du jeune artiste Terence Lin, diplômé de l'Académie des Beaux-Arts de Nanyang. Deux salles privées sont également à disposition des convives.

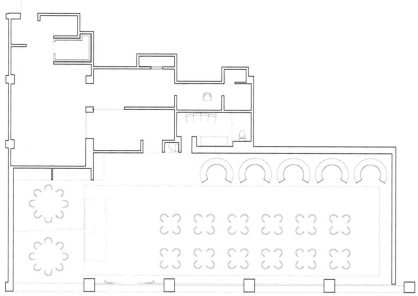

Namus Boutique Restaurant

Seongnam, South Korea

Alpha-mighty Bldg 6F, Seohyeon-dong, Bundang-gu
Seongnam, 463-824

Phone: +82 317 060 069
www.namus.co

Prices: $$
Cuisine: Korean

Architecture/Design
CHIHO & Partners
www.chihop.com

Photos
Kim Young/Indiphos

In Korean, "namu" means wood, which is why interior designer Chiho Kim highlighted this material in the restaurant. Inspired by scenery from Fritz Lang's classic silent movie "Metropolis," Kim conjures a geometric and futuristic setting for his wood theme. He also developed a complex lighting concept to visually break up the 9,600-square-foot restaurant with its nearly 30-foot ceilings. As a result, the bar seems to float thanks to the LED lighting from below. Projecting down from the ceiling, an angular lighting installation reminiscent of stalactites sets the scene. Backlit elements are also mounted on walls and the ceiling. Booths with seat backs over six feet high make up some of the seating options. Guests who prefer more privacy can choose to eat in private dining rooms, where they can enjoy the Korean cuisine prepared in the open kitchen.

„Namu" bedeutet auf Koreanisch Holz, weshalb Innenarchitekt Chiho Kim dieses Material in den Fokus rückte. Ihm schwebte eine Szenerie aus Fritz Langs Stummfilmklassiker „Metropolis" vor, sodass das Thema Holz eine geometrische und futuristisch wirkende Umsetzung erfuhr. Um das gut 900 Quadratmeter große und neun Meter hohe Restaurant optisch zu unterteilen, hat er ein komplexes Beleuchtungskonzept entwickelt. So wirkt die Bar fast schwebend, da sie von unten durch LEDs angestrahlt wird. Von der Decke setzen rechteckige, an Stalaktiten erinnernde Leuchten den Raum in Szene. Auch an den Wänden und der Decke finden sich hinterleuchte Elemente. Die Sitzplätze sind teilweise durch Bänke mit gut zwei Meter hohen Rückenlehnen abgetrennt. Wer noch ungestörter essen will, kann die in der offenen Küche zubereiteten koreanischen Gerichte auch in privaten Dining-Räumen zu sich nehmen.

« Namu » signifie « bois » en coréen, ce qui explique sans peine pourquoi l'architecte d'intérieur Chiho Kim s'est largement servi de ce matériau. Il s'est principalement inspiré du film muet « Metropolis » de Fritz Lang, de sorte que le bois se retrouve au cœur d'un concept géométrique et futuriste. Il a également développé un système d'éclairage complexe afin de proposer une division optique de ce restaurant de 900 mètres carrés et neuf mètres de haut. Illuminé par le bas à l'aide de LEDs, le bar donne ainsi l'impression de flotter. Des lampes carrées faisant penser à des stalactites pendent du plafond, équipé tout comme les murs d'autres jeux de lumière. Certaines tables sont séparées par des bancs dont le dossier s'élève à deux mètres de hauteur. Si vous désirez encore plus d'intimité, vous pouvez déguster les plats coréens préparés dans une cuisine ouverte dans l'une des salles à manger privées.

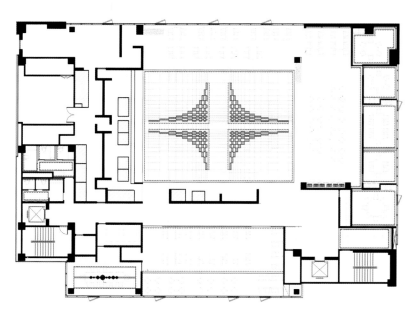

Neni am Naschmarkt

Vienna, Austria

Naschmarkt 510
Vienna, 1060

Phone: +43 1 585 2020
www.neni.at

Prices: $
Cuisine: Oriental Bistro

Architecture/Design
Eva Beresin
www.beresin.com

Photos
Martin Nicholas Kunz (3)
courtesy of Neni (1)

On the second floor of Neni, guests feel like they are in the belly of a ship because the walls of the former market stall arch overhead and meet at the peak. The wooden roof beams and the exposed ventilation pipes running along the ceiling create a certain industrial charm. Eva Beresin is the Viennese artist behind the interior design of Neni. She has filled the space with sleek wooden furniture paired with white Thonet chairs to compliment the restaurant's Oriental menu. In the courtyard, guests sit at traditional bistro furniture in the shade of an olive tree. Across the way is Neni's second market stall with even more room for guests and a striking "box" containing the restroom: It is constructed with concrete embedded with fiber optics and has massive sliding doors made of wood.

Wie im Bauch eines Schiffes fühlt man sich in der ersten Etage vom Neni. Denn die Wände des früheren Marktstands sind oval nach oben gewölbt. Für Industrie-charme sorgen die freigelegte Holzkonstruktion des Daches und die unter der Decke verlaufenden sichtbaren Belüftungsrohre. Den Innenausbau verantwortet die Wiener Künstlerin Eva Beresin. Sie hat das Restaurant mit der orientalischen Speisekarte mit schlichtem Holzmobiliar ausgestattet und dazu weiße Thonet-Stühle kombiniert. Im Hof sitzen die Gäste unter einem Schatten spendenden Olivenbaum auf traditionellen Bistromöbeln. Gegenüber befindet sich der zweite Marktstand des Nenis mit noch mehr Platz für Gäste und der auffälligen „Toilettenbox": Sie ist aus mit Glasfasern durchsetztem Beton gebaut und hat massive Schiebetüren aus Holz.

Le premier étage du restaurant Neni pourrait faire penser à la cale d'un navire. Les murs voûtés de cette ancienne échoppe de marché se dressent vers le plafond dans une forme ovale. Le toit, parsemé de poutres en bois, et les tuyaux d'aération visibles du plafond confèrent à l'endroit un charme industriel. L'aménagement intérieur de ce restaurant aux saveurs orientales est l'œuvre de l'artiste viennoise Eva Beresin, qui a opté pour un alliage de chaises blanches Thonet et de mobilier en bois simple. Dans la cour extérieure, les clients se restaurent à l'ombre de l'olivier, sur des sièges traditionnels de bistro. La deuxième échoppe de Neni se trouve en face et dispose d'encore plus d'espace pour accueillir les convives. Sa fameuse « boîte aux toilettes », construite en béton et fibre de verre et dotée de portes coulissantes en bois massif, se charge d'attirer l'attention de la clientèle.

Plachuttas Gasthaus zur Oper

Vienna, Austria

Walfischgasse 5–7
Vienna, 1010

Phone: +43 1 512 2251
www.plachutta.at

Prices: $$
Cuisine: Austrian

Architecture/Design
Atelier Heiss
www.atelier-heiss.at

Photos
Philipp Kreidl
courtesy of Atelier Heiss

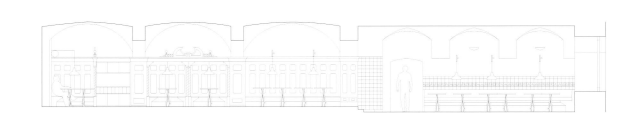

The restaurant of well-known Austrian restaurateur Mario Plachutta combines traditional with urban elements. Like a stylized homage to Viennese inns, the interior connects the rooms of two houses, parts of which are under landmark protection. The architects of Atelier Heiss blended handcrafted elements such as tile reliefs and wall panels with wooden furniture reminiscent of Scandinavian minimalistic design. Custom-designed solid wood tables with crossed metal legs resembling dancers reference the nearby Vienna State Opera and its ballet. Enameled pendant lights with industrial charm shed the proper light on classic Wiener schnitzel and seasonal specialties. In the summer, a terrace that seats 150 is an inviting place to enjoy the original Viennese brewery beer in the shade of the awning.

Im Restaurant des bekannten österreichischen Gastronomen Mario Plachutta finden Tradition und urbane Ansprüche zueinander. Wie eine stilisierte Hommage an das Wiener Gasthaus verbindet das Interieur die teilweise denkmalgeschützten Räume zweier Häuser. Die Architekten von Atelier Heiss kombinierten kunsthandwerkliche Elemente wie Fliesenreliefs und Wandvertäfelungen zu Holzmobiliar, das an skandinavisches Minimaldesign erinnert. Als Verweis auf die Nähe zur Staatsoper und deren Ballett stehen die eigens angefertigten Massivholztische auf sich „tänzerisch" kreuzenden Metallbeinen. Konsequent eingesetzte Emaille-Hängeleuchten mit industriellem Charme setzen klassisches Wiener Schnitzel und saisonale Spezialitäten ins rechte Licht. Im Sommer lädt eine Terrasse mit 150 Plätzen ein, das original Wiener Brauereibier im Schatten der Markise zu genießen.

Dans le restaurant du célèbre gastronome autrichien Mario Plachutta, tradition et exigences urbaines se marient parfaitement. L'intérieur de cet établissement viennois relie avec style deux maisons, dont certaines pièces sont protégées à titre de monument historique. Les architectes de l'Atelier Heiss ont combiné des éléments artisanaux tels que du carrelage en relief et des boiseries avec du mobilier en bois, qui rappelle le design minimaliste scandinave. Afin d'évoquer la proximité avec l'opéra national et son ballet, les tables en bois massif, faites sur mesure, reposent sur des pattes métalliques qui s'entremêlent comme si elles dansaient. Les plafonniers en émail savamment disposés permettent de mettre en lumière les escalopes viennoises et autres spécialités de saison. En été, une terrasse de 150 places vous invite à déguster une bière viennoise à l'ombre de la marquise.

166 Plachuttas Gasthaus zur Oper

Long March Canteen

Berlin, Germany

Wrangelstraße 20
Berlin, 10997

Phone: +49 178 884 9599
www.longmarchcanteen.com

Prices: $$
Cuisine: Chinese

Architecture/Design
ett la benn
www.ettlabenn.com

Photos
ett la benn

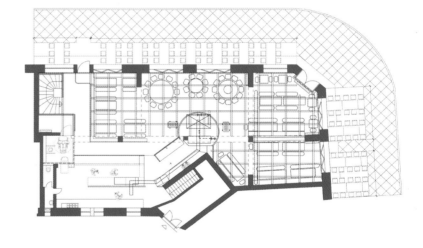

A dark side entry leads to the restaurant's dimly lit entrance, where a blue neon sign confirms to diners that they have arrived at the Long March Canteen. After passing by wooden blinds concealing the kitchen, guests enter an atmosphere of steaming dim sum baskets, Asian fragrances, and busy staff in uniforms. LED downlights illuminate black tables, while metal lanterns hanging from wooden ceiling beams bring to mind scenes from Chinese backyards. Once guests have been seated, wait staff offer appetizers from serving carts and then use an iPad to send orders directly to the kitchen. Dim sum, dumplings, and exotic specialties from the menu invite diners on a flavorful journey through Southeast Asia. It is not until they leave the restaurant that visitors remember that they are still in Berlin.

Ein dunkler Seiteneingang führt in das spärlich beleuchtete Entree des Restaurants, wo eine blau leuchtende Neonschrift dem Besucher bestätigt: Long March Canteen. Vorbei an Holzjalousien, hinter denen sich die Küche abzeichnet, betritt der Gast eine Atmosphäre aus dampfenden Dim-Sum-Körben, asiatischen Gerüchen und geschäftigem Personal in Uniformen. LED-Downlights erhellen schwarze Tische, während von der Holzbalken-Decke hängende Metalllaternen an chinesische Hinterhofszenen erinnern. Ist der Gast platziert, offeriert die Bedienung Vorspeisen vom Servierwagen, um dann die Bestellung mithilfe eines iPads direkt an die Küche zu senden. Dim Sum, Dumplings und exotische Spezialitäten der Speisekarte laden zu einer geschmacklichen Reise durch Südostasien. So mancher Besucher merkt erst beim Verlassen des Restaurants, dass er sich noch immer in Berlin befindet.

Une entrée latérale sombre mène à l'accueil modestement éclairé du restaurant, où un néon bleu indique au visiteur qu'il se trouve bien au Long March Canteen. Après avoir passé les persiennes en bois derrière lesquelles se cache la cuisine, l'invité pénètre dans une atmosphère où se mêlent les vapeurs de dimsum, les odeurs asiatiques et le personnel vêtu d'uniformes. Des spots LED éclairent les tables noires tandis qu'au plafond, les lanternes métalliques accrochées aux poutres en bois rappellent les arrière-cours chinoises. Une fois le convive bien installé, le serveur vient offrir des entrées sur son chariot, avant de passer commande à la cuisine directement depuis un iPad. Les dimsums, boulettes et spécialités exotiques du menu invitent à un voyage gustatif en Asie du Sud-Est. Ce n'est alors qu'en quittant l'établissement que le visiteur s'aperçoit qu'il se trouve encore à Berlin.

Sage Restaurant

Berlin, Germany

Köpenicker Straße 18–20
Berlin, 10997

Phone: +49 30 755 494 071
www.sage-restaurant.de

Prices: $$
Cuisine: Fusion

Architecture/Design
Drewes und Strenge
www.drewesstrenge.com

Photos
diephotodesigner.de

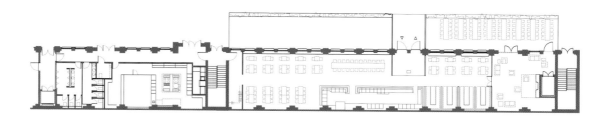

Berlin is known for its night clubs at least as much as it is for its currywurst, so it was just a matter of time until club scene protagonists decided to mix things up in the world of gastronomy. With their restaurant concept, the operators of the established Sage Club have added an unusual twist to the sophisticated cuisine available in Berlin. With house classics such as beef tartare or Wiener Schnitzel, eccentric pizzas, and a changing evening menu influenced by haute cuisine, Sage Restaurant is as diverse as its clientele. A colorful mixture of people from the worlds of art, design, and media gather to dine in this formerly industrial brick building, and the atmosphere is casual. The clear highlight in the summer is the outdoor area directly along the Spree River, which offers a beach bar, a terrace with a barbeque, and a DJ playing music.

Für seine Nachtclubs ist Berlin mindestens genauso bekannt wie für seine Currywurst, und so war es nur eine Frage der Zeit, bis einige Protagonisten der Club-szene die Gastronomielandschaft aufmischten. Die Betreiber des etablierten Sage Clubs erweitern mit ihrem Restaurantkonzept auf ungewöhnliche Weise Berlins Angebot gehobener Küche. Mit Haus-Klassikern wie Beef Tatar oder Wiener Schnitzel, ausgefallenen Pizza-Kompositionen und einer wechselnden Abendkarte mit Einflüssen der Haute Cuisine präsentiert sich das Sage Restaurant so facettenreich wie seine Klientel: Ein bunt gemischtes Volk aus Kunst, Design und Medien-branche trifft sich zum Essen in einem ehemals industriell genutzten Backsteingebäude, die Atmosphäre ist leger. Highlight im Sommer ist der Außenbereich, der eine Strandbar, eine Terrasse mit Grill und DJ-Sounds direkt an der Spree zu bieten hat.

Berlin est aussi connu pour ses boîtes de nuit que pour sa currywurst. Ce n'était donc qu'une question de temps avant que certains acteurs de la vie nocturne ne décident d'envahir le paysage gastronomique. Les gérants du Sage Club ont ainsi décidé d'ouvrir un restaurant, qui complète l'offre en haute cuisine de la ville de manière innovante. Le Sage Restaurant propose les classiques steaks tartare ou escalopes de Vienne, mais aussi des pizzas insolites ainsi qu'une carte du soir sans cesse renouvelée et aux accents de grande cuisine. Le menu comporte ainsi presque autant de facettes que la clientèle. Cette dernière regroupe des professionnels de l'art, du design et des médias qui aiment à se retrouver dans ce vieux bâtiment industriel en briques et à l'atmosphère légère. En été, l'espace extérieur offre un bar et une terrasse au bord de la Spree, où vous pourrez profiter de grillades et de la musique du DJ.

Lacrimi si Sfinti

Bucharest, Romania

Strada Sepcari 16
Bucharest, 030116

Phone: +40 372 773 999
www.lacrimisisfinti.com

Prices: $$
Cuisine: Modern Romanian

Architecture/Design
Corvin Cristian
www.corvincristian.com

Photos
Cosmin Dragomir (6)
Corvin Cristian (1)

The restaurant's furnishings feel like they were made by an art collector with a tendency toward nostalgia and a love for children's toys. The walls are decorated by folkloristic borders, tapestries, hunting trophies and other curiosities, all created from Lego pieces by artist Ionel Brânzoi. Architect Corvin Cristian plays with humorous details: A workbench is refashioned into a bar table, dishes are stored in antique kitchen cabinets mounted against a wall, and when guests go to freshen up, they can decide which of the nine mirrors above the wash basin they wish to use. Always a bit tongue-in-cheek and just as humorous as the interior design is the menu, which features modern Romanian dishes including "Sentimental Catfish" and "Pick-me-up Soup." For those who don't know: Lacrimi si Sfinti means "tears and saints."

Die Einrichtung des Restaurants wirkt wie das Werk eines Kunstsammlers mit einem Hang zur Nostalgie und einer Vorliebe für Kinderspielzeug. Die Wände zieren folkloristische Bordüren, Gobelins, Jagdtrophäen sowie andere Kuriositäten, die Künstler Ionel Brânzoi allesamt aus Legobausteinen zusammengesetzt hat. Architekt Corvin Cristian spielt mit humorvollen Details: So wird eine Werkbank zum Stehtisch umfunktioniert, ein Stapel antiker Küchenschränke dient als Geschirr-Lager und der Gast muss sich beim Frischmachen für einen der neun Spiegel über dem Waschtisch entscheiden. Stets mit einem Augenzwinkern und ebenso stimmig wie das Design präsentiert sich die Speisekarte mit modernen rumänischen Gerichten, darunter der „Sentimental Catfish" oder die „Pick-me-up Soup". Lacrimi si Sfinti bedeutet übrigens Tränen und Heilige.

La décoration du restaurant fait penser au repaire d'un collectionneur d'art un brin nostalgique et amoureux des jouets pour enfants. Les murs sont en effet ornés de moulures, tapisseries, trophées de chasse et autres curiosités, toutes réalisées en pièces de Lego par l'artiste Ionel Brânzoi. L'architecte Corvin Cristian s'amuse pour sa part avec les détails : un établi est transformé en table haute, d'antiques meubles de cuisine servent de range-vaisselle et lorsqu'un convive veut aller se rafraîchir, il doit choisir parmi les neufs miroirs qui trônent au-dessus du lavabo. Le menu multiplie lui aussi les clins d'œil et se marie parfaitement au design. Il propose des plats roumains modernes, parmi lesquels le « Sentimental Catfish » et la « Pick-me-up Soup ». Lacrimi si Sfinti signifie par ailleurs Larmes et Saints.

Mandarin Oriental Paris

Paris, France

251, rue Saint-Honoré
Paris, 75001

Phone: +33 1 70 98 73 00
www.mandarinoriental.com/paris

Prices: $$$$
Cuisine: French-Asian

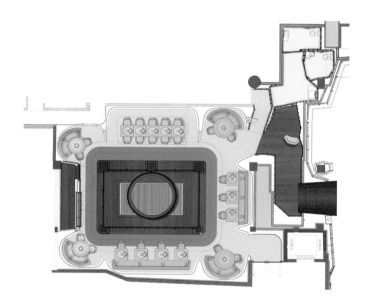

Architecture/Design
Jouin Manku Studio
www.jouinmanku.com

Photos
Hélène Hilaire
courtesy of Mandarin Oriental

Patrick Jouin and Sanjit Manku wanted to capture the emotions of Paris in their design for both restaurants, Camélia and Sur Mesure, and the Bar 8 of the Mandarin Oriental. The establishments are interconnected through a lushly landscaped interior courtyard. Natural materials from the garden are repeated in the interior spaces: Wood veneers are used extensively on the walls and in the bar. Striking wall elements—some reminiscent of oversized camellia petals, others consisting of torn strips of material—set the scene in some of the backlit sitting areas. Thanks to their unusual surfaces, they break up the monochromatic appearance of the space. Head of the kitchen at Mandarin Oriental is chef Thierry Marx, recipient of two Michelin stars; his name stands for innovative French cuisine combined with Asian-Pacific influences.

Patrick Jouin und Sanjit Manku wollten die Emotionen von Paris auffangen, als sie die beiden Restaurants, Camélia und Sur Mesure, und die Bar 8 des Mandarin Oriental gestalteten. Die Lokalitäten sind durch einen üppig bepflanzten Innenhof miteinander verbunden. Natürliche Materialien aus dem Garten finden sich auch in den Innenräumen: So sind die Wände und die Bar größtenteils mit Holzfurnier versehen. Auffällige Wandelemente, die mal an überdimensionale Kamelien-blütenblätter erinnern, mal aus zerfetzten Stoffbahnen bestehen, setzen einige der hinterleuchteten Sitzecken in Szene. Durch ihre ungewöhnlichen Oberflächen durchbrechen sie den einfarbigen Look des Raumes. Die Küche des Mandarin Oriental ist unter der Leitung des mit zwei Michelin-Sternen ausgezeichneten Chef-kochs Thierry Marx – sein Name steht für innovative französische Kochkunst mit asiatisch-pazifischen Einflüssen.

Patrick Jouin et Sanjit Manku ont cherché à reproduire les émotions parisiennes dans l'aménagement des deux restaurants, Camélia et Sur Mesure, et du Bar 8 du Mandarin Oriental. Les salles sont reliées par une cour intérieure luxuriante dont certains matériaux naturels ont été utilisés pour la décoration intérieure. Ainsi, les murs et le bar sont constitués en grande partie de bois plaqué. D'impressionnants éléments muraux, comme des pétales de camélia surdimensionnés ou des panneaux de tissus déchirés, permettent de mettre en valeur certaines tables à l'éclairage indirect. Leur surface inhabituelle contraste en outre avec la sobriété unie de l'ensemble de la pièce. Le maître des fourneaux du Mandarin Oriental n'est autre que le grand chef Thierry Marx, doublement étoilé au Michelin et connu pour sa cuisine française novatrice aux influences pacifico-asiatiques.

La Corde à Linge

Strasbourg, France

2, place Benjamin Zix
Strasbourg, 67000

Phone: +33 3 88 22 15 17
www.lacordealinge.com

Prices: $$
Cuisine: Alsatian

Architecture/Design
P. Claude Drach/my Beautiful
www.mybeautiful.fr

Photos
P. Claude Drach
www.mybeautiful.fr

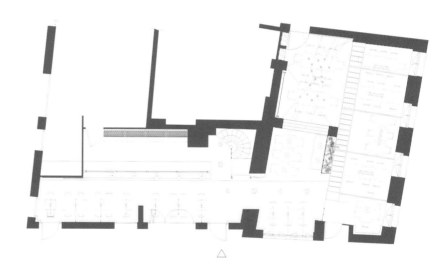

Designer Pascal Claude Drach took the ground floor of two buildings, located between the city's former laundries, and transformed it into a café and restaurant with a blend of styles rich in detail. The bar area, which features mostly dark tones, was inspired by 1930s art deco French brasseries. By contrast, the dining area is mainly white and cleverly weaves in laundry themes. The historic neighborhood and the designer's scenographic work experience are apparent in the overall concept for the furnishings. An authentic atmosphere is created through nostalgic compositions of notions, slightly industrial furniture, and the eponymous clothesline along with pieces of laundry hanging from it. Even the cuisine refers to the establishment's history: Original Alsatian specialties, such as meatballs and Munster cheese, are given creative names from the textile industry.

Designer Pascal Claude Drach hat das Erdgeschoss zweier Gebäude, gelegen zwischen den früheren Waschhäusern der Stadt, in ein Café und Restaurant mit einem detailreichen Stilmix verwandelt. Vom Art déco französischer Brasserien der 30er Jahre ist der dunkel gehaltene Bar-Bereich inspiriert. Im Kontrast dazu greift der weiß gehaltene Gastraum das Thema Wäscherei auf. Die historische Nachbarschaft und die szenographische Arbeitserfahrung des Designers lassen sich im gesamten Einrichtungskonzept erkennen. Arrangements nostalgischer Kurzwaren, industriell anmutendes Mobiliar und die namengebende Leine, inklusive daran hängender Wäsche, sorgen für eine authentische Atmosphäre. Auch die Küche unterstreicht den lokalen Bezug mit original elsässischen Spezialitäten wie Fleischkechles und Münsterkäse, die auf der Karte allesamt Namen aus dem Textiljargon tragen.

Le designer Pascal Claude Drach a transformé le rez-de-chaussée de deux bâtiments, situés entre les anciens lavoirs de la ville, en un café-restaurant proposant un mélange stylistique riche en détails. Le bar sombre s'inspire de l'Art déco des brasseries françaises dans les années 30. Tout en contraste, la salle de restaurant parée de blanc rappelle l'héritage des lavoirs. Le décor historique avoisinant et l'expérience de la mise en scène du designer se reconnaissent parfaitement dans l'aménagement global des lieux. Une atmosphère d'authenticité se dégage des arrangements nostalgiques de mercerie, du mobilier à l'aspect industriel ainsi que du fil auquel du linge est immanquablement étendu. La cuisine est pour sa part locale, avec des spécialités alsaciennes originales telles que les Fleischkechles ou le munster, qui dans le menu portent toutes des noms se référant au jargon du textile.

Kødbyens Fiskebar

Copenhagen, Denmark

Flæsketorvet 100
Copenhagen, 1711

Phone: +45 32 15 56 56
www.fiskebaren.dk/en

Prices: $$$
Cuisine: Seafood Grill

Architecture/Design
SPACE Copenhagen
www.spacecph.dk

Photos
courtesy of Kødbyens Fiskebar

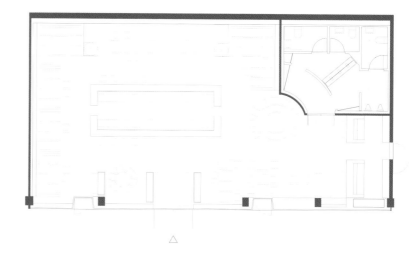

An enormous statue of a bull is a reminder of the days when huge quantities of meat were processed every day in the Copenhagen meatpacking district. Today, the industrial buildings of White Meat City are home to hip clubs, bars, and restaurants, such as Kødbyens Fiskebar. Some of the restaurant's furnishings consist of found materials or were simply left in their original state, and with their patina they break up the sterile atmosphere of the loft space. A bar made of brushed metal and old varnished wooden door panels with barstools custom-made to match form the heart of the interior. The highlight is a round saltwater aquarium that bathes the room in blue light. As might be surmised from the name, fish and seafood are the primary components in the creations by head chef Anders Selmer, the former sous-chef at renowned Michelin-star restaurant Noma.

Eine enorme Stierstatue erinnert an Zeiten, in denen im Kopenhagener „Meatpacking District" noch täglich Fleisch in Massen verarbeitet wurde. Heute befinden sich in den Industriegebäuden der „White Meat City" angesagte Clubs, Bars und Restaurants wie Kødbyens Fiskebar. Teile der Einrichtung bestehen aus vorgefundenen Materialien oder wurden im Originalzustand belassen und brechen mit ihrer Patina die sterile Atmosphäre des Loftraumes. Ein Bartresen aus gebürstetem Metall und alten lackierten Holztürbrettern mit eigens dafür gestalteten Hockern bildet das Herzstück des Interieurs. Highlight ist ein rundes Salzwasseraquarium, das den Raum in blaues Licht taucht. Wie der Name vermuten lässt, sind Fisch und Meeresfrüchte Hauptbestandteil der Kreationen von Küchenchef Anders Selmer, dem ehemaligen Souschef des bekannten Sterne-Restaurants Noma.

Une énorme statue de taureau rappelle l'époque où les bouchers régnaient en maîtres sur le « meatpacking disctrict » de Copenhague. Aujourd'hui, les bâtiments industriels de la « White Meat City » sont occupés par des boîtes de nuit, bars et restaurants en vogue, parmi lesquels Kødbyens Fiskebar. Certains éléments de la décoration sont des matériaux d'époque ou ont été laissés dans leur état original, et la patine permet de briser l'atmosphère stérile du loft. Le véritable joyau de l'établissement est le comptoir du bar, en métal brossé et planches de bois laqué, pour lequel des tabourets ont été fabriqués sur mesure. La salle est plongée dans une lumière bleutée par un aquarium d'eau de mer rond. Ainsi que le nom le laisse suggérer, le poisson et les fruits de mer sont la base des créations du chef Anders Selmer, ancien second du célèbre restaurant étoilé Noma.

Barbican Foodhall and Lounge

London, United Kingdom

Silk Street (Barbican Centre)
London, EC2Y 8DS

Phone: +44 20 7638 4141
www.barbican.org.uk/restaurants-bars

Prices: $$
Cuisine: International

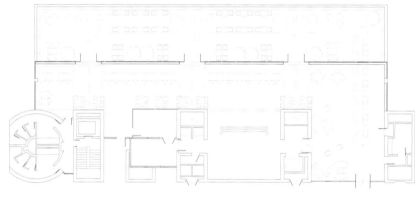

Architecture/Design
SHH & .PSLAB
www.shh.co.uk, www.pslab.net

Photos
Gareth Gardner

The architectural firm SHH has set up a restaurant on the ground floor of the Barbican Centre. In an area resembling a supermarket, visitors can purchase food and drinks to go. Plants and huge custom-made umbrellas separate the terrace from the sidewalk, and the brick floor provides a visual connection to the outdoors. .PSLAB designed the lighting concept for the restaurant. The lighting designers and manufacturers chose to use a mixture of oversized light bulbs on the massive exposed concrete ceilings and angular lighting modules of their own creation over the counter and the buffet. The Barbican Foodhall features a blend of custom furniture, vintage pieces, and design classics.

Im Erdgeschoss des Kultur- und Konferenzzentrums The Barbican hat das Architekturbüro SHH ein Restaurant eingerichtet. In einem supermarktähnlichen Bereich gibt es Essen und Getränke zum Mitnehmen. Die Terrasse ist durch Pflanzen und maßgefertigte Riesenschirme vom Gehweg getrennt. Eine optische Verbindung nach außen stellt der mit Backsteinfliesen gepflasterte Boden her. Für das Beleuchtungskonzept des Restaurants ist das Büro .PSLAB verantwortlich. Die Licht-designer versahen die extra freigelegten, massiven Betondecken teils mit überdimensionalen Glühbirnen, teils mit eigens kreierten, eckigen Leuchtmodulen über dem Tresen und dem Buffet. Eingerichtet ist The Barbican Foodhall mit einer Mischung aus speziell angefertigten Möbeln, Vintage-Stücken und Designklassikern.

Le cabinet d'architectes SHH a aménagé le rez-de-chaussée du centre culturel et de conférence « The Barbican » en un restaurant, où un espace aux allures de supermarché propose également de la cuisine et des boissons à emporter. La terrasse verdoyante est séparée de l'allée piétonnière par d'énormes parasols. Les pavés du sol en briques se chargent de créer l'illusion d'optique d'un chemin vers l'extérieur. L'aménagement lumineux est l'œuvre de l'entreprise .PSLAB qui a su mettre en valeur le plafond en béton dégarni, à l'aide d'une part d'ampoules surdimensionnées, et d'autre part de modules lumineux carrés de propre création, accrochés au-dessus du bar et du buffet. La décoration intérieure du Barbican Foodhall combine des meubles sur mesure, des pièces vintage et des classiques du design.

196 Barbican Foodhall and Lounge

Alemàgou

Mykonos, Greece

Ftelia Beach
Mykonos, 84600

Phone: +30 694 443 7343
www.alemagou.com

Prices: $$
Cuisine: Greek

Architecture/Design
K-Studio
www.k-studio.gr

Photos
Yiorgos Kordakis

With architecture that falls between the traditional and contemporary, Alemàgou confidently fits into its idyllic beach location on Ftelia Beach on Mykonos. Here, the architectural style typical for the Cyclades—rounded corners, whitewashed façades, drystone walls, and gourd lamps—encounters the cosmopolitan flair of a vacation island. The innovation is in the details: An organically shaped floor made of cast concrete seamlessly transforms into benches made of the same material and contrasts with an airy reed-thatched roof that provides shade. During the day, Alemàgou is a popular café for vacationers and local surfers; in the evenings, you can enjoy the lounge atmosphere over Greek food, or simply order a drink at the bar and sip it under the open sky.

Mit einer Architektur zwischen Tradition und Moderne passt sich das Alemàgou stilsicher in das Strandidyll des Ftelia Beach auf Mykonos ein. Der für die Inselgruppe der Kykladen typische Baustil – mit abgerundeten Ecken, weiß getünchten Fassaden, Trockensteinmauern und Kalebassen-Lampen – trifft auf das kosmopolitische Flair der Urlaubsinsel. Die Innovation liegt im Detail: Ein organisch geformter Boden aus Gießbeton geht fließend über in Sitzbänke aus gleichem Material und kontrastiert zu einer luftigen Deckenkonstruktion aus getrocknetem Schilf, die für Schatten sorgt. Tagsüber ist das Alemàgou ein beliebtes Café bei Urlaubern und einheimischen Surfern, abends genießt man bei Lounge-Atmosphäre griechisches Essen oder nimmt einen Drink an der Bar unter freiem Himmel.

L'Alemàgou et son architecture alliant tradition et modernité s'intègrent avec assurance à la plage idyllique de Ftelia, à Mykonos. Le style si typique des îles des Cyclades, avec ses coins arrondis, ses façades blanches, ses murs en pierre sèche et ses lampes calebasse, est joliment adapté à l'ambiance cosmopolite de cette île touristique. Les innovations sont toutes entières dans les détails : un sol organique en béton et des bancs du même matériau contrastent avec le toit en roseau séché, qui fournit à la fois de l'air frais et de l'ombre. La journée, l'Alemàgou est un café très apprécié des vacanciers et des surfeurs locaux, tandis qu'en soirée, vous pourrez profiter de la cuisine grecque ou d'un verre au bar à ciel ouvert, le tout dans une atmosphère lounge.

Chan at The Met Hotel

Thessaloniki, Greece

26th October Street 48
Thessaloniki, 54627

Phone: +30 231 001 7000
www.themethotel.gr

Prices: $$$
Cuisine: Asian

Architecture/Design
Andy Martin Architects
www.andymartinarchitects.com

Photos
Vangelis Paterakis
www.studiopaterakis.com

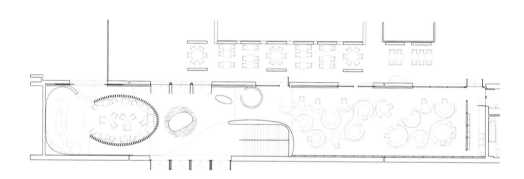

When guests enter the restaurant in the Met Hotel, they are immersed in a perfectly staged atmosphere. The award-winning lighting design by Andy Martin is based on LED technology and outlines shapes reminiscent of a bamboo grove on the walls and bars. Design elements with touches of Far Eastern aesthetics and a carpet design inspired by manga comics are allusions to Asian street culture, which interior designer Andy Martin became familiar with while traveling through Hong Kong, Thailand, and Indonesia. The lighting selectively illuminates round tables separated by padded partition walls, creating a feeling of privacy. The overall concept is rounded out by a pan-Asian menu put together by gastronomy expert Oliver Peyton, which has made Chan into one of the most popular restaurants in the city.

Beim Betreten des Restaurants im Met Hotel taucht der Gast in eine perfekt inszenierte Atmosphäre ein. Die auf LED-Technik basierende Lichtgestaltung von Andy Martin ist preisgekrönt und spielt an Wänden und Bartresen mit Formen eines stilisierten Bambushains. Gestaltungselemente mit Zitaten fernöstlicher Ästhetik und das von Manga-Comics inspirierte Teppichdesign sind Anlehnungen an asiatische Straßenkultur, die Designer Andy Martin während seiner Inspirations-reisen nach Hongkong, Thailand und Indonesien kennengelernt hat. Gezielt beleuchtete Rundtische, die von gepolsterten Zwischenwänden getrennt sind, schaffen Privatsphäre. Abgerundet wird das Gesamtkonzept von einer pan-asiatischen Speisekarte, zusammengestellt von Gastronomie-Koryphäe Oliver Peyton, was das Chan zu einem der angesagtesten Restaurants der Stadt macht.

En franchissant la porte du restaurant du Met Hotel, l'invité plonge dans une atmosphère tout à fait particulière. La conception lumineuse à base de LEDs, créée par Andy Martin, a été primée et trace sur les murs et le comptoir du bar une forêt de bambous. Certains éléments à l'esthétique extrême-orientale ainsi que les tapis inspirés de l'univers des mangas rappellent la culture de rue asiatique, découverte par le designer Andy Martin lors de ses voyages à Hong Kong, en Thaïlande et en Indonésie. Des tables rondes savamment éclairées et séparées par des cloisons rembourrées apportent une touche d'intimité. L'ensemble est complété par un menu pan-asiatique imaginé par Oliver Peyton, monstre sacré de la gastronomie, qui fait du Chan l'un des restaurants les plus prisés de la ville.

204 Chan at The Met Hotel

Troll Wall Restaurant

Åndalsnes, Norway

Horgheimseidet
Åndalsnes, 6300

Phone: +47 958 98 045
www.visit-trollveggen.com

Prices: $
Cuisine: Fast-Food

Architecture/Design
Reiulf Ramstad Arkitekter
www.reiulframstadarkitekter.no

Photos
courtesy of Reiulf Ramstad Arkitekter

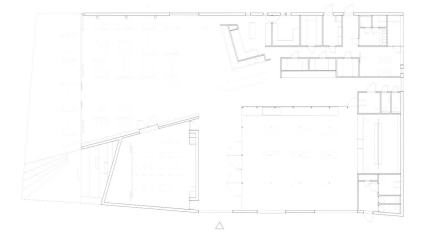

Architect Reiulf Ramstad has constructed a jagged glass structure at the foot of the Troll Wall, the highest vertical rock face in Europe. Located in the Romsdalen valley in Norway, the Troll Wall has majestic peaks that are reflected in the roof's shape. In 2009, Ramstad's design was selected for the new visitor center encompassing a restaurant, tourist information, auditorium, and gift shop. The side of the building facing the rock wall is all glass; at first glance, it appears to have been built into the rock itself. To one side of the exterior are cantilevered wooden stairs. The restaurant area features exposed white wooden beams in geometrical patterns, with the same zig-zag pattern repeated in the chair backs. Under the high ceiling, naked light bulbs bathe the room in light.

Einen zackigen Glasbau hat Architekt Reiulf Ramstad am Fuße der Trollwand, der höchsten vertikalen Steinwand Europas, errichtet. Sie befindet sich im norwegischen Romsdal-Tal mit seinen majestätischen Gipfeln, die in der Dachform des Baus nachempfunden sind. Ramstads Entwurf gewann 2009 die Ausschreibung für das neue Besucher-Center mit Restaurant, Touristen-Information, Auditorium und Souvenirladen. Das Gebäude ist zur Felsenwand hin verglast, sodass es auf den ersten Blick so aussieht, als sei es in den Stein gebaut. Daneben ist eine Freitreppe aus Holz angegliedert. Sichtbare, weiße Holzbalken in geometrischen Mustern bestimmen den Restaurant-Bereich. Die Zick-Zack-Muster finden sich in den Stuhllehnen wieder. Nackte Glühbirnen unter der hohen Decke tauchen den Raum ins rechte Licht.

Cette construction en verre au toit dentelé a été conçue par l'architecte Reiulf Ramstad au pied du Trollveggen, la plus haute paroi rocheuse verticale d'Europe. Elle est située dans la vallée de Romsdal, dont les sommets majestueux se reflètent dans la forme du toit. Ramstad a remporté en 2009 un appel à projets pour ce nouveau centre de visiteurs comptant un restaurant, un office du tourisme, un auditoire et une boutique de souvenirs. L'édifice en verre et bois, construit le long de la paroi rocheuse, donne l'illusion d'être ancré dans la pierre. L'escalier en bois attenant vous emmène sur ses hauteurs. Des poutres blanches en bois, aux formes géométriques, déterminent l'espace du restaurant dont les chaises présentent des motifs en zigzag sur leurs dossiers. Le tout est agrémenté d'ampoules nues qui dévoilent la salle sous son véritable visage.

La Terraza del Casino

Madrid, Spain

Calle de Alcalá 15
Madrid, 28014

Phone: +34 91 532 12 75
www.casinodemadrid.es

Prices: $$$$
Cuisine: Molecular

Architecture/Design
HAYONSTUDIO
www.hayonstudio.com

Photos
Nienke Klunder

This restaurant on the roof of the Casino de Madrid has been a culinary institution since its inception in 1998. Like his former mentor Ferran Adrià, head chef and cookbook author Paco Roncero belongs to the avant-garde of molecular gastronomy, a field whose mission is to push the boundaries of traditional cooking and redefine it. The visionary spirit and aesthetics of Roncero's edible masterpieces are also reflected in the redesigned interior by Hayon Studio. Star designer Jaime Hayon took the grandeur of the architecture of this protected building constructed in 1903 and reinterpreted it with his unmistakable style of lacquered surfaces, cubist shapes, and playful objects. Hayon put his stamp on every detail of the furnishings, from the chandeliers to the wall mirrors to porcelain dolls.

Bereits seit 1998 ist das Restaurant auf dem Dach des Casino de Madrid eine kulinarische Institution. Küchenchef und Kochbuch-Autor Paco Roncero gehört wie sein ehemaliger Mentor Ferran Adrià zur Avantgarde der Molekularköche, die es sich zur Aufgabe gemacht haben, die Grenzen des traditionellen Kochhandwerks auszuloten und neu zu definieren. Der visionäre Esprit und die Ästhetik von Ronceros essbaren Kunstwerken spiegeln sich auch in der Umgestaltung des Interieurs durch das Hayon Studio wider. Stardesigner Jaime Hayon hat die Grandezza der denkmalgeschützten Architektur des 1903 erbauten Gebäudes aufgegriffen und mit seinem unverkennbaren Stil aus gelackten Oberflächen, kubistischen Formen und verspielten Objekten neu interpretiert. Ob Kronleuchter, Wandspiegel oder Porzellanpuppe – jedes Einrichtungsdetail ist seiner Feder entsprungen.

Le restaurant situé sur le toit du casino de Madrid est une institution depuis 1998 déjà. Le chef Paco Roncero, auteur de livres de cuisine par ailleurs, compte parmi les avant-gardistes de la cuisine moléculaire en compagnie de Ferran Adrià, son ancien mentor. Ces cuisiniers cherchent à repousser et redéfinir les limites traditionnelles de l'art culinaire. L'esprit visionnaire de Roncero ainsi que l'esthétique de ses plats se retrouvent également dans l'aménagement intérieur, réalisé par le studio Hayon. Le célèbre designer Jaime Hayon a parfaitement su intégrer la splendeur de l'architecture de ce bâtiment protégé, construit en 1903. Il a même su la réinterpréter avec son style inimitable, à grands renforts de surfaces laquées, de formes cubistes ou de poupées en porcelaine, et le moindre détail porte indubitablement son sceau.

Griffins' Steakhouse Extraordinaire

Stockholm, Sweden

Klarabergsviadukten 67
Stockholm, 11164

Phone: +46 08 5450 7647
www.griffinssteakhouse.se

Prices: $$$
Cuisine: Steakhouse

Architecture/Design
Stylt
www.stylt.se

Photos
Erik Nissen Johansen

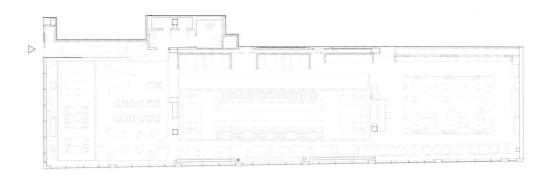

Interior designers from Stylt drew inspiration for the concept of this location from an invented love story: A mad scientist, based on the "Invisible Man" Griffin, a character from an H.G. Wells novel, meets a dancer à la Josephine Baker in a library in 1920s Paris, and they fall in love. Their shared penchant for the eccentric is reflected in a strange ambience combining alchemy and Moulin Rouge, which rightly gives Griffins' Steakhouse its attribute "extraordinaire." Laboratory equipment and natural history antiques represent his world, while her influence is seen in heavy velvets, vaudeville lamps, and portraits of famous dancers. Wing chairs and stacks of old books lend the restaurant a library atmosphere. Fitting in perfectly with its eclectic furnishings, the restaurant offers a fusion of French cuisine, classic grilled dishes, and Scandinavian seafood specialties.

Die Inspiration der Designer von Stylt für das Konzept dieser Location war eine erdachte Liebesgeschichte: Ein verrückter Wissenschaftler, angelehnt an den „Invisible Man" Griffin, eine Romanfigur von H.G. Wells, und eine Tänzerin à la Josephine Baker treffen im Paris der 20er Jahre in einer Bibliothek aufeinander und verlieben sich. Ihr gemeinsames Faible für Ausgefallenes spiegelt sich in einem eigenartigen Ambiente aus Alchemie und Moulin Rouge, das Griffins' Steakhouse zurecht sein Attribut „extraordinaire" verleiht. Laborutensilien, naturhistorische Antiquitäten repräsentieren seine Welt, schwerer Samt, Varieté-Lampen und Portraits bekannter Tänzerinnen stehen für ihren Einfluss, während Ohrensessel und Stapel alter Bücher eine Bibliotheksatmosphäre schaffen. Passend zur eklektischen Ausstattung bietet das Restaurant eine Fusion aus französischer Küche, Klassikern vom Grill und skandinavischen Spezialitäten aus dem Meer.

Dans cet établissement, les designers de la maison Stylt ont inventé une histoire d'amour. Un savant fou inspiré du personnage de Griffin dans « L'Homme invisible » de H.G. Wells et une danseuse à la Joséphine Baker se rencontrent dans une bibliothèque parisienne des années 20 et tombent amoureux. Leur faible pour l'excentricité est retranscrit dans une ambiance singulière mêlant les mondes de l'alchimie et du Moulin rouge. Le qualificatif « d'extraordinaire » du Griffins' Steakhouse est ainsi loin d'être usurpé. Ustensiles de laboratoire et objets d'histoire naturelle représentent son monde à lui, tandis que le velours lourd, les lampes extravagantes et les portraits de danseuses célèbres sont de son influence à elle. Les fauteuils à oreilles et les piles de vieux livres créent également une atmosphère de bibliothèque. Le menu lui aussi est éclectique et allie cuisine française, grillades classiques et spécialités maritimes scandinaves.

Editor	Martin Nicholas Kunz Raphael Guillou	
Texts	Raphael Guillou Judith Jenner	
Copy Editing	Dr. Simone Bischoff	
Editorial Management	Sina Milde	
Creative Direction	Martin Nicholas Kunz	
Layout & Prepress	Sophie Franke	
Photo Editing	David Burghardt	
Imaging	Tridix, Berlin	
Translations		
English	Heather Bock Romina Russo	
French	Samantha Michaux Romina Russo	

Published by teNeues Publishing Group

teNeues Verlag GmbH + Co. KG
Am Selder 37, 47906 Kempen, Germany
Phone: +49 (0)2152 916 0, Fax: +49 (0)2152 916 111
e-mail: books@teneues.de

Press department: Andrea Rehn
Phone: +49 (0)2152 916 202
e-mail: arehn@teneues.de

teNeues Digital Media GmbH
Kohlfurter Straße 41–43, 10999 Berlin, Germany
Phone: +49 (0)30 700 77 65 0

teNeues Publishing Company
7 West 18th Street, New York, NY 10011, USA
Phone: +1 212 627 9090, Fax: +1 212 627 9511

teNeues Publishing UK Ltd.
21 Marlowe Court, Lymer Avenue, London SE19 1LP, UK
Phone: +44 (0)20 8670 7522, Fax: +44-(0)20 8670 7523

teNeues France S.A.R.L.
39, rue des Billets, 18250 Henrichemont, France
Phone: +33 (0)2 4826 9348, Fax: +33 (0)1 7072 3482

www.teneues.com

© 2012 teNeues Verlag GmbH + Co. KG, Kempen

ISBN: 978-3-8327-9628-0
Library of Congress Control Number: 2012932115

Printed in the Czech Republic

Bibliographic information published by
the Deutsche Nationalbibliothek.

The Deutsche Nationalbibliothek lists this publication in
the Deutsche Nationalbibliografie; detailed bibliographic
data are available in the Internet at http://dnb.d-nb.de.

Photo Credits
On first page of each restaurant, excepting:

Cover photo by Paul Rivera/archphoto
Back cover photo by Nacása & Partners Inc.

p. 2 (Griffins' Steakhouse Extraordinaire) by Erik Nissen Johansen
p. 3 and p. 9 (Delicatessen) by David Joseph
p. 4 (Alemàgou) by Yiorgos Kordakis
p. 5 (Hōtō Fudō) by Koji Fujii/Nacása & Partners Inc.
p. 6 (Tori Tori) by Paul Rivera/archphoto
p. 10 (Lacrimi si Sfinti) by Cosmin Dragomir/courtesy of Lacrimi si Sfinti
p. 220 (Blue Frog) by Fram Petit